SEND ME I'LL GO

$\longleftarrow \rangle|\bullet|\langle \longrightarrow$

Preparing for the Call

♡ genevieve

GENEVIEVE DAWN

Trilogy Christian Publishers
A Wholly Owned Subsidiary of Trinity Broadcasting Network
2442 Michelle Drive
Tustin, CA 92780

Cover design by: Cornerstone Creative Solutions

For information, address Trilogy Christian Publishing
Rights Department, 2442 Michelle Drive, Tustin, Ca 92780.
Trilogy Christian Publishing/ TBN and colophon are trademarks of Trinity
Broadcasting Network.

For information about special discounts for bulk purchases, please contact
Trilogy Christian Publishing.

Manufactured in the United States of America

10 9 8 7 6 5 4 3 2 1

Library of Congress Cataloging-in-Publication Data is available.

ISBN 978-1-63769-092-5 (Print Book)
ISBN 978-1-63769-093-2 (ebook)

Dedication

This book is dedicated with much love to Jesus, my King. You did not have to rescue me from my captivity, but You did.

To every child, past, present, and future who has come through the doors of NAOMI House and all children who have been separated from their families, under any circumstances.

To the staff of NAOMI House who have laid down their lives to serve the Lord, in selfless dedication. May you reap a thousand times and even more for your seed sown into the lives of children.

My prayer is for every reader to encounter their Savior and experience a personal revival in their own life that will impact many generations to follow in many ways.

Endorsements

—————————————➤)•(←—————————————

"At first glance, *Send Me, I'll Go; Preparing for the Call,* Genevieve's title of her new book, should be held in high regard. After all, these are Isaiah's of the Bible, his very own words answering God's call to serve.

"What resonated even more, for me, was that kind of 'life offering service,' in the preface, was tied to the words of Billy Graham's speech to a gathering of Native Americans back in 1975. He alluded to Native Americans as a 'spiritual superpower.'

"The following pages will lead you, the reader, in God's very own plan that many have accepted and experienced for themselves. Now you can be a witness to not only Genevieve's spiritual path but be prepared to behold for your own God's supernatural plan to call you, fill you, then pour you out for the benefit of those to which you will be called.

"It will be seen through the personal testimony of Ms. Skidmore's Spirit-filled life in serving our Creator God, and now all you have to do is to believe that God can do what He says He will do. "And Jesus said to him, 'If you can! All things are possible for one who believes.' Immediately the father of the child cried out and said, 'I believe; help my unbelief!'

"Prophetically, the late Billy Graham's words gave our people hope. Could it be that God will use First Nations to help bring about the next great revival, as well as restore His original intent in First Nations People? To be a modern-day

Spiritual Superpower to bring new messages of healing and reconciliation to spiritually dry and starving land.

"In this book, all of the ingredients are in place for you to partake—all you have to do is Prepare for the Call and be willing to go wherever God will send you!"

—Mr. Myron Lizer, Navajo Nation Vice President

"This book is long overdue. A testimony for the world of what Jesus can do in and through one life. Through the eyes of an Indigenous woman of God, this book is a landmark!"

—Pastor Quincy Good Star, Grace City Church, Rapid City, South Dakota

"*Send Me, I'll Go* is more than a must-read—it is the last days marching orders for all those hungry to experience transformation at a national level! Genevieve has been given a great Kingdom strategy and carries the passion and the wisdom to see what is contained in the pages of this book become a reality!"

—Pastor Daniel Williamson, Church for the Nations, Flagstaff, Arizona

"*Send Me, I'll Go* is a passionate narrative that pulls the curtain back on what life is like on America's Reservations. The author, a member of the Lakota Sioux Tribe of South Dakota and a missionary to First Nations children in Arizona, discloses eye-opening and shocking first-hand accounts, historical facts, and Scriptural truths. Everyone isn't called to be a missionary, but all Christians are called to missions. *Send Me, I'll Go* highlights a mission field that is crying out for Jesus right in our own backyard. This book will challenge, inspire, and equip you to fulfill your call."

—Gloria Brintnall, Author, Speaker, Assistant
Pastor, Faith4life Church, Dallas, Texas

Acknowledgments

I want to thank everyone who has encouraged me and covered me in prayer during the writing of this book, especially Ms. Ann Waters and Apostle Fred Smith. I want to genuinely say thank you for all the years of heartfelt intercession and spiritual covering for me and my family.

To Ms. Linda Thompson for responding in faith to God's call to Arizona and laying the foundation for NAOMI House for generations to come. Special thanks to my newfound brother in Christ, Mr. Tom Steffen. Your step-by-step guidance, through a simple request, means more to me than you may know. Thank you for your heart for the global mission field. Thank you for humbly offering your expertise to a brand-new author.

A big shout-out to my little sister Jessica. I honestly don't know what I would do without your friendship. Your sense of humor and laughter are like medicine to my soul. You have been my ride-or-die battle buddy through the many ups and downs, highs and lows of life, motherhood, and ministry. I thank God for you.

To my big sister Jennifer, for your continual support and encouragement. Thank you for being a tangible expression of Christ's love to me, all of your nieces and nephews, and all those who know you.

And finally, to my mother, Susan Sharon. Thank you for opening up your heart to our Lord and Savior, Jesus

Christ, while I was yet in your womb. Your years of crying out to Father God on behalf of your daughters surely did not fall upon deaf ears. The best is yet to come!

Contents

Foreword

"Within the pages of this amazing book, Genevieve has captured the very heart of God's redemptive plan for the lives of our Native people. Isaiah 61:1-3 testifies to the very fact that God's plan, His desire, and His will, is to bind up the brokenhearted, proclaim liberty to those found captive, to open prison doors. Jesus came to help the less fortunate and overlooked in life rise above and beyond the ashes of life's most difficult tragedies. We can now exchange life's sorrows into praise and triumph, as He anoints us with fresh oil, plants and cultivates our lives, transitioning us into the newness of His precious Life, all the while filling us with His very essence. What an amazing book filled with real-life stories from real-life people, and real-life situations. This is a book filled with practical applications on how to live life in an abundant manner. Thank you, Genevieve, for sharing your heart with us, for allowing God's redemptive plan for your life to manifest, and for helping all those that have the same desire, to rise above. You really are an amazing woman of God."

—Apostle Fred Smith, First Nation
Ministries, Ft. Duchesne, Utah

Preface

In 1975, Billy Graham gave an iconic speech at a conference on Indian evangelism, saying to Native American leaders, "You as Indians are a sleeping giant. You are now awakening. You may become a spiritual superpower in this country that can change not only America but the world."

A line in Greg Miller's film, *Awakened*, reads, "If we believe that the things Billy Graham stated forty plus years ago are coming to fruition right now, then getting behind this movement, and inspiring first Americans to take their place in Jesus is arguably the single most important thing we can do as believers!"[1]

Ron Hutchcraft Ministries, one of the largest organizations targeting Native American Youth, puts it like this: "There is a battle raging for a generation of young men and women, and the winner of that battle *owns the future of this nation.* This generation needs someone who will respond to the cries of the spiritually dying and who will *leave their safe place and go* where lost young people are."

I have a burden to raise awareness around the subject of Native American children in need, as well as a burden to help prepare those called to the frontlines of ministry. For those who are called with a kingdom advancing mandate to a people group that is not their own, I pray this book is a helpful, equipping tool.

This is my story of awakening, arising, and responding to kingdom purpose, reaching back to a generation, all for His Glory. Let this book be a reminder that we are *not* disqualified or defined by the sorrows and pains of the past. Truly where the enemy attempted to wound beyond repair is where the anointing of God flows most powerfully. Our story is our message. It is a testimony of *resilience* because of the sovereignty of God. If the enemy has tried to silence you, it is only because it is *your* voice that carries a unique sound, a frequency that has the potential to unlock spiritual freedom.

As Native Americans from every tribe and tongue are arising to find their strategic place in the Body Christ, they *can* lead this nation into true revival. I sense an urgency to sound the alarm and *rally the awakened warriors* to circle up for this next move of God.

God is calling all of His people into the battle that is taking place now—at the frontlines. Can you hear the call? *Are you able to support those who do?*

Kingdom purposes are not accomplished by accident or default. It will take an army made up of seasoned warriors and kingdom enforcers who are committed to walk in humility and see honor restored.

For anyone who is ready to step up and into your assignment, it is essentially a warzone. Here, everything in your life will be put to the test—your mind, your emotions, your marriage and family, your belief systems, and cultural views—*all* tested.

No military soldier would ever enter the battlefield without any training. Boot camp is strenuous and challenging, but the lessons learned there can save your life and the lives of others.

Let us be ever reminded that in the midst of all adversity, "overwhelming victory is ours through Christ" (Romans

8:37, NLT). We are representatives of heaven, enforcing God's original plans and purposes in the earth, confidently and securely rooted in God's living Word (Hebrews 4:12).

Let this book inspire the Church, equip the first responder, and stir the zeal and fire of all people! It is time to arise and mobilize! God has need of *you!*

Introduction

Years ago, I experienced a radical encounter with God. I don't know any other way to describe it but to liken it to Paul on the road to Damascus. It was as if the power of God literally fell upon my life so suddenly and forcefully that even my own free will was overridden as I stood under the conviction, mercy, and forgiveness of a living God. I knew at that moment that the rest of my life would be taking a radically different course.

Sin separates us from our Father, who is Life and Light. We were made to live in close proximity to Him. Apart from Him, there is only death and darkness. What I didn't realize was that Jesus Christ is *the way* that reconnects me to my Creator. Not church. Not religion. Not tradition. Not culture or deep theology. Not guilt, shame, or condemnation. But one *encounter* with the Man they call Jesus *can* transfer you from the Kingdom of Darkness to the Kingdom of Light.

When the power of God hit my life, I had an immediate revelation of absolute forgiveness and God-given purpose. I became acutely aware that we have not only been saved; we have also been called.

> "Who has *saved us and called us*
> with a holy calling, not according to our
> works, but according to His own purpose

and grace which was given to us in Christ Jesus before time began."

2 Timothy 1:9 (NKJV, emphasis added)

Wow! Even before time began, God *chose me* to *save* and *call*.

The word *save* is an amazing word with deep and powerful meaning! *"Saved"* means so much more than a resurrected life after death or to live in heaven for eternity (not to take away from that, because that surely would be enough, period). But the word *save* in the original Greek is the word *sozo,* which means *rescued, delivered, healed, and made whole!* If there was one thing I was painfully aware of, it was that I was broken. I wanted this promise of wholeness in my life more than I wanted anything else.

Not only did God *save* me, He *called me. Called* means *to name and give an attribute or assign a quality to for a specific purpose.* I was determined to do whatever it took to search out this plan, this purpose, this call. I attended Bible School and soaked up, like a dry sponge, all the teaching, preaching, and training that I could.

Only a couple of years after God reached into the deep darkness of my life and power-punched me with purpose, I knew without a doubt that He was calling me out of one place into another. I knew way down deep that my calling was back to the First Nations people.

I didn't have the vocabulary for it then, and I certainly wouldn't have considered the term "missionary" to describe God's call on my life. But come to find out, He *saved* me and *called me* to *send me.* For me, that sending was to Northern Arizona just minutes from the Navajo Reservation to a little placed called NAOMI House—a safe house for Native American children in need.

—Genevieve

PART I

Send Me, I'll Go

"In the year that King Uzziah died, I saw the
Lord sitting on a throne, high and lifted up,
and the train of His robe filled the temple.
Above it stood seraphim; each one had six
wings: with two he covered his face,
with two he covered his feet, and with two he flew.
And one cried to another and said:
"Holy, holy, holy is the Lord of hosts; The
whole earth is full of His glory!"
And the posts of the door were shaken by
the voice of him who cried out,
and the house was filled with smoke.
So I said: "Woe is me, for I am undone!
Because I am a man of unclean lips,
And I dwell in the midst of a people of unclean lips;
For my eyes have seen the King, The Lord of hosts."
Then one of the seraphim flew to me,
having in his hand a live coal
which he had taken with the tongs from the altar.
And he touched my mouth with it, and said:

"Behold, this has touched your lips; Your iniquity
is taken away, And your sin purged."
Also I heard the voice of the Lord, saying:
"Whom shall I send, And who will go for
Us?" Then I said, *"Here am I! Send me."*
And He said, *"Go,* and tell this people."

Isaiah 6:1-9b (ESV)

1

Generation Now

"There will be descendants who serve him,
a generation that will be told about Adonai."

~Psalm 22:30 (NOG)~

One evening I was driving home with a ten-year-old boy. In the few months that he and his younger siblings had lived with us, we had never talked much about where he came from or why he was placed with us in our children's home. We have found that if we do not put too much emphasis on any one child or situation as they come into the new family dynamic, they are able to adjust to a "new temporary normal" much easier.

On this very rare occasion, it was just he and I in the car. As we were driving that night, he began to share his story, and my heart broke—one more time. I learned that his mother had been "cut with an ax" on her arm one night by his intoxicated father while the children looked on. Every adult in the house was under the influence.

"Where is he, your father, now?" I asked. "Dead." He replied very bluntly. He continued, "His girlfriend gave him some kind of drug when he came out of prison, and it killed him."

"Don't your two siblings have different dads?" I asked, trying to act like that wasn't the most devastating news I'd ever heard. Well, at least since the story of the child before. "Yes," he answered, "he's in prison though because he raped his girlfriend and killed her."

Looking back on that evening, driving in the car, listening to another child's story, I realized he said it all so matter-of-fact-like and with almost no emotion. It sent chills down my spine as I remembered the gravity of the phrase I often use and think I comprehend when I say it:

> *"The realities of growing up Indigenous in America today are very different than in most other cultures and people groups. Beneath the resilience and beauty of the First Nations people lies extreme peril, and often, unspeakable trauma that harshly affects the most vulnerable of all— the children!*

Over the years, hundreds of children have come through the NAOMI House doors. The following stories can be very difficult to hear, but I share them because it is the daily reality of many families.

When the founder of NAOMI House, Ms. Linda, went to pick up a six-month-old baby, Andrea, in White River (Apache), she called me on the way home with the new little bundle. She began, "Sister, we got us a punkin! But, there's something terribly wrong with the left side of her body. It's delayed." When she arrived with baby Andrea, all I saw were big, beautiful, brown eyes staring back at me. She was simply a gorgeous baby girl. It wasn't until later that we were told what happened.

Andrea was born perfectly normal to her fourteen-year-old mother. At three weeks old, her mom and dad got into a drunken brawl, and mom threatened dad: "If you leave me, I'm going to throw her down on the pavement." *Dad left.* Andrea suffered a serious brain injury that leaves her partially paralyzed on one side of her body, as well as damage in the frontal lobe part of her brain that affects her ability to process emotionally.

Instead of crawling, Andrea scooted on her little right leg and bottom to get around. After years and years of living with us and a load of doctors and therapists, Andrea was adopted by Linda. She is sixteen now.

Her mother sat in jail for many years; her dad died at the very young age of twenty-three due to alcohol poisoning and liver failure. The difference with Andrea is that, unlike the rest of the children, her trauma is clear for all to see on the outside. Each one of these kids has battle wounds, scars, and pain that may not be visible to the eyes but are imprinted deep within the human soul, spanning generations deep. (see Photo #1 on page 240)

> The difference with Andrea is that,
> unlike the rest of the children,
> her trauma is clear for all to see on the outside.

One day social services called to let us know that there were three small boys—brothers between the ages of one to five—who needed placement. There was a lot of drug and alcohol use in the home. The boys lived with us for about a year, having sporadic visits from a very beat-down, meth-addicted momma who loved her boys very much.

One Friday afternoon, the social worker called to say she would be picking the boys up that day to return to mom! This is always welcome news, as reunification is always the goal. However, the following Monday, the social worker brought the boys back for placement. Over the weekend, the two-year-old was murdered by mom's boyfriend. The domestic violence incident was meth-related. The grief and confusion of the five-year-old were obvious and heartbreaking as he walked around our house asking for his little brother over and over, "Where's my Joseph?"

Seven-year-old Lita had second-degree burns over a third of her body when she came to NAOMI. Her mother and aunt had lit her on fire because they said she had a "demon." They were both high on meth at the time.

Crystal, a very bright and mature thirteen-year-old, came to us with her three-month-old baby. The father of the baby was her stepdad. She was molested and raped for years and became pregnant at twelve years old. Besides how beautiful and perfect her little baby was, the thing that sticks out to me about Crystal was that at just thirteen years old, she was an incredible mother! She didn't want the staff to take care of her baby, she wanted to do it, *and she did!* Very well, I might say. I was simply amazed at her resilience. Amazed by all of them, really.

For me, our beloved Brian is one of the reasons I am writing this book. I remember the look in his eyes as he sat on the chair across my desk at just thirteen years old. His eyes were like a deep tunnel that went on and on forever in a lost emptiness. He was so very precious, so very wounded.

He loved his family and wanted to be home. He did his very best to encourage his two younger brothers to "behave" while they all lived with us. He always inquired about "going home" and about his mother and family. He would ask his social worker: "How about now? Can I go home now?" Each time, to no avail. No running water at home or electricity. Poverty was one reason for so much alcohol addiction in the home. Or perhaps it was the other way around? I don't know. All I know is that he desperately loved his family.

Brian eventually ended up connecting on deep levels with every one of us, but especially with my bio son, Josh. They had become just like brothers. Brian looked up to Josh, and Josh cherished their friendship. He was getting ready to turn eighteen, and I'm telling you, his bags were packed to finally return to his family that day in mid-December. His social worker advised against it. Even when we pleaded with him to stay until May to graduate high school, it was obvious his mind was made up. He understandably missed his family and wanted to return to the reservation as he had spent his whole life in the foster care system.

Methamphetamines found Brian shortly after returning to the reservation. It was a quick spiral down, and two years later, our beloved Brian committed suicide. He hung himself on his family's property. He left a precious two-year-old son, Jacob, behind, who looks just like his handsome daddy. (see Photo #2 on page 240)

I could go on and on, story after story. Just when I felt I had heard the worst atrocity, here comes the next one, or two or three, or as a sibling group. This book is a discussion regarding First Nations people and children, from the perspectives of my own experiences and testimony, and certainly not to say there aren't problems that manifest in many different ways and forms in the whole country and the world. The severe issues that I am addressing are not isolated to the Navajo Nation or White Mountain Apache Tribes. No. These atrocities are affecting *almost every reservation* in America. In fact, in 2015, the Oglala Lakota Sioux Tribe issued a national state of emergency because of the high rate of suicide amongst the Lakota youth. And again, in 2019, there was a state of emergency declared because of the overwhelming devastating effects of meth upon reservation families and meth-induced homicides. These are the realities of which others are unaware—the realities that need our attention, voice, and response. I take tremendous encouragement in this; God has not forgotten about His people.

Frederick Douglass rightly concludes, "It's easier to build strong children than to repair broken men." That's why NAOMI House was begun.

Located in Northern Arizona, NAOMI House (Native American Outreach Ministries, Inc.) is dedicated to providing a safe and loving home to Native American Children in need since 1993.

NAOMI House is contracted by the Navajo Nation as an Emergency shelter for twelve children and licensed as a long-term foster care for ten children. The current full-time missionary staff includes six adults and twenty-six children. Our largest-scale dream is that each of these children be reunified with their biological families in a safe and loving environment. Until then, NAOMI House and its incredible staff, donors, and countless volunteers serve on the front lines around the clock, 365 days a year. Our thirty-day emergency shelter has an average stay of two years. We turn away approximately four children a month due to a lack of space on our current property.

NAOMI House welcomes children into a "one big family" environment. There is a constant and reliable schedule that the kids can depend on, along with lots of love, laughter, singing, and Bible devotions. The children have access to regular and general healthcare through the local IHS (Indian Health Care Center). This is also where they receive any necessary counseling or psychiatric care. We have maintained the structure and foundation of a home-like atmosphere as begun by our founder, Ms. Linda. The following is an excerpt from her own words:

Meet our Founder of NAOMI House, Ms. Linda Thompson (see Photo #3 on page 241)

In the fall of 1985, the Lord called me (Linda) to Arizona from Kentucky to work with Native American Children. The children's extreme trials and obstacles only increased my burden for them. Experiencing the pain of sexual abuse firsthand while living here gave me a new insight and burden for these precious children. More than anyone I had ever met, these innocent ones needed to know the healing love of Jesus Christ. NAOMI was established in 1993, and we moved into our Children's Home in January of 1995.

We are told that it takes a village to raise a child. However, when a child has been abused and wounded, it takes more than just one village—it takes many. NAOMI is one small village, working with many others to help hurting children recover from child abuse.

Native American children suffer from abuse at one of the most alarming rates in our country. Child sexual abuse in Native America is both epidemic and holocaustic. Ninety percent of the children that come to live at NAOMI House are the victims of child molestation.

My (Linda's) heart's desire, and the reason NAOMI exists, is to share the healing love of Jesus Christ with hurting children that desperately need His healing touch. NAOMI was established as a non-profit home for abused and neglected Native American children.

"We at NAOMI strive to maintain an atmosphere that not only looks like home but also feels like home. We are a family. We are not a boarding school or dormitory. For the sake of the children, we avoid all appearances of an institution and endeavor to be as culturally appropriate as possible.

Meeting the diverse and complicated needs of sexually abused children as soon as they have been hurt enables them to heal and come to terms with their abuse. We aspire to help end child molestation one child at a time by removing wounded children from the vicious cycle that led to their abuse."

Linda was invited to work with the children on the Navajo Nation after meeting a couple from Northern Arizona at a Christian conference in Kentucky. When she saw Pastors Roy and Mag Begay across the room, she made a bee-line over to them, asking them where they were from. They told her all about Arizona and the need for Christian ministry there. Linda's early years in Arizona consisted of living in a Hogan with the Begay family and Grandma Eskee, where she became a student of the people God had called her to serve. (see Photos #4 and #5 on page 241)

Linda started as a dorm mom at a boarding school for a time and eventually married a Navajo Pastor. Her story is full of faith and power and would require a second book, which I am urging her to write. By God's grace, her legacy continues and is impacting countless lives.

My Introduction to NAOMI House

When I arrived to serve all those years ago, I remember Linda handing me the ministry checkbook. She said, "Pay all the bills in full when they come," and she walked out. Honestly, I have been doing that ever since. Somehow, in some way, God has always provided financially for this ministry. Half of our annual budget is received through our tribal contract and license, emergency shelter, and foster care. The other half comes through many small, monthly donations made by faithful individuals and churches with a heart for the children. Our full-time missionary staff of six is paid a small monthly stipend and resides on-site. God takes precious care of His babies, and to witness His financial miracles and provision has been truly amazing.

At the time that I met Linda, NAOMI House consisted of herself, a total of 11 children, and Jesus. That's it! No staff, no buildings. Even before Facebook and Social Media, Linda had a unique gift to rally people together for a cause. She had such a contagious faith that exuded from her. She trusted God, period. The children loved her tenderly, and it was just one big, beautiful, messy family. In all of the chaos in this unorthodox family dynamic, one thing was abundantly clear—the Presence of the Lord was in this place. An indescribable peace permeated the fabric of the home in a hectic, circus kind of way! *The Fathers' love for his beautiful children on full display, NAOMI House is a front-row seat to the miraculous.* This is because where you see suffering, where you see languishing, pain, and injustice, you will find Jesus there. It's where you will find Him—in the dirt with the hurting.

> The Father's love for his beautiful children on full display, NAOMI House is a front-row-seat to the miraculous.

I will never forget that first-weekend visit with Linda, whom I endearingly call the crazy white lady from Kentucky or Momma Linda. I showed up in her office and explained, "I really don't know exactly why I'm here." I shared with her that I was a member of the Oglala Sioux Tribe, originally from South Dakota, and how I had experienced a power encounter with God. I explained that I knew beyond a doubt that God had called me to spread the Good News to my Native brothers and sisters! God is real! Jesus is actually who He says He is. He has a plan! There is hope!

She prayed with me and encouraged me to do everything God had for me in life. I said, "Well, I guess I'll go clean something," as I knew I would only be here for the weekend.

The next morning, we were driving out to the reservation to attend church at Black Rock with Grandma Eskee. On the way there, Linda turned and looked at me. She said, "I had a dream about you." I was like, woah. I knew her all of twenty-four hours. At that moment, she prophesied. She said, "I believe God has called you here to learn how to run NAOMI House so that you can take it to South Dakota one day." Woah! Deep down, I knew that it was true.

Shortly thereafter, I packed up my bags in Phoenix, and my nine-year-old son and I responded to God's call. I had the nerve in my naivety to tell God, "I'll give you one year." I remember genuinely thinking to myself. Man, He really hit the jackpot! I'm going to give Him a whole year! He didn't listen. That was fifteen wild years ago and so much in between to say. *A NAOMI House, South Dakota², serving the Oglala Sioux children, families, and community is now a very real opportunity.*

When I first realized many years ago that I was called to "the ministry," I somehow glamorized it a bit in my mind.

God had to show me that what you do for Him behind the scenes far outweighs the few moments in front of people, and I promise you that was a long, painful death process for the flesh. I can honestly say I would not have chosen "children's ministry" or group homes. Nope. However, after He pulled me up out of the power of darkness, turned on the lights, healed me down to my shattered soul, and then healed me in my physical body, I had determined to serve Him however it looked. I said, "God, You really are who You say You are. You can do what You say You can do. I will go where You want me to go."

As a first responder, there is so much one will learn. When you give God your "yes," there is really no way of understanding what you are signing up for. The statement Paul made will become your reality: "I die daily. I am crucified with Christ; it is no longer I that lives." This type of "yes" requires a hit on all levels of the spectrum—extreme highs and extreme lows.

As I look back on that first weekend, as well as the first portion of my new NAOMI House life, I kept thinking, "God, why am I here? I can't do this. I don't know what I'm doing. These kids have way more needs than I have the capacity." I was overwhelmed by the spectrum of emotion involved when working in a high-stress, high-needs environment. It was pure compassion mixed with helplessness. Anger and frustration followed, and then here would come absolute joy and contentment, just as suddenly!

Countless times and I mean countless times, I would come to the firm determination this is definitely *not* for me. God bless them all though, they'll be fine. God can use someone else who is way more qualified, more compassionate, more patient, and certainly more equipped.

Reflecting back on that first weekend before returning to my life in Phoenix, I remember we all sat down in the living room to have devotions together. One particularly difficult child was seven-year-old Jeremiah. Man! He was just out of control, on meds, and just so fractured emotionally. He was a lot of work; he had me completely spent in one weekend, and there were eleven more just like him.

That night at devotions, Linda started the now-familiar tune. She would sing, "I got my mind made up! And my heart is fixed! I'm going with Jesus all the way!" Then all of the children's voices would chime in to repeat, "We got our minds made up, and our hearts are fixed, we're going with Jesus all the way!" I looked over at Jeremiah. He had the biggest smile on his face singing his little heart out about how he had made up his mind to go with Jesus all the way, and I broke.

As they sang, my mind wandered to his particular story that Linda had shared. Jeremiah's father, while highly intoxicated, stabbed and hung his mother, who, believe it or not, survived the domestic violence and attempted murder.

There were such conflicting thoughts swarming around in my soul. "God, I can't. God, I don't want to. God, no!" Linda finished the song with "and Who is The Way?" And everyone shouted *"Jesus!"*

After just one weekend at NAOMI House, I knew that I couldn't be the same. I didn't know what saying "yes" meant. I had no way of knowing what I was getting ready to step into. What I did know was that I was called to Native American ministry, and I knew that God was in this place.

Concluding Reflections

There is an untold number of stories, countless children, where these have come from.

The precious ones noted in this brief chapter are simply a representation of a very vast demographic across the fabric of our countries Native American Reservations. I applaud, honor, and deeply admire each one. Their stories are providing a connecting point, a context, for the rest of society, whereby we can hold an imperative conversation in this nation regarding our children.

Truly to honor their stories and declare their hopeful future is, to begin with, sharing my own.

2

Called Out of Darkness

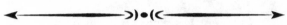

"He brought them out of darkness and the shadow of death,
and broke their chains in pieces."

~Psalm 107:14 (NKJV)~

At the writing of this book, I have served at NAOMI House
and worked with the beautiful children for over fifteen years.
It was only within the last several years that I really felt a
God-given burden to raise national awareness of the plight
of Native American children. What I quickly realized was
that one could not raise awareness about the children without raising awareness about Native American people in general. If I am going to speak about these subjects, the question
becomes, *who are you?*

The number one question I am asked is: "Why do
you work here at NAOMI House?" Besides the fact that I
responded to His call to do so, the reasons I am so passionate
about being a voice in the wilderness are: 1) because of what
Native American children are exposed to on a daily basis, and
2) because of a personal experience in the miracle-working,
power of God to transform.

You see, I, too, was caught up in many of the statistical issues that I am discussing and addressing in my own
life. If it had not been for a direct encounter with Jesus, my
own children would have entered the foster care system, or

worse. Through the power of my praying mother, He broke me loose from the bonds of wickedness and gave me a voice to shout from the rooftops: *"There is hope! God still saves, heals, and delivers!"*

> "He sent His word and healed them,
> and delivered them from their destructions."
>
> ~Psalms 107:20 (NKJV)~

Born and raised in South Dakota, I am a member of the Oglala Lakota Sioux Tribe on my mothers' side.

My grandparents owned quite a bit of land on the reservation that was used to harvest wheat. Growing up, we spent time there. As a young girl, I never consciously thought of the idea of going on and off the reservation. It was just a normal occurrence. In fact, it wasn't until I was in my 20s that I realized that there were other natives besides Lakota!

My aunt lived on my grandparents' land until she died. My mother lived with her while attending the Oglala Lakota College in Pine Ridge, where she received her nursing degree after my two sisters, and I graduated from high school.

Though I grew up in a small South Dakota town about an hour away from the Pine Ridge Reservation, I did not escape the common issues that plague the people. My people. Your people. Many people. My father (Caucasian) died at the young age of fifty-three. After a lifetime of drug and alcohol abuse, his body and heart had had enough, and he died in his sleep. In spite of all his many shortcomings and hang-ups, I loved him dearly and miss him daily.

I don't know if you remember the "Jesus Movement?" The Spirit of God was poured out on those crazy hippies in the late 70s. That outpouring stretched all the way into the Midwest and straight into the soul of my pregnant mother. She received salvation in Jesus and was baptized in the Holy Spirit. She was eight weeks pregnant with me.

It was her third pregnancy without being married, so mom and dad decided they would have an abortion. My mother recounts that on arrival at the clinic, when my dad got out of the car, there was a bright light that shone down on him. He immediately turned around and got back into the car. They were married soon after. My life was spared that day. My mother says that she doesn't remember having one "sober" conversation with my father before she said, "I do." And there wouldn't be many afterward.

My parents began their new life together. My dad always struggled with addiction, drugs, and alcohol. He had the mentality that if a little is good, a lot is better. My mom was a new Christian convert with a wounded soul. She was not only coping with the trauma of her own childhood but also carried the overwhelming weight of an emotionally incapacitated, alcoholic husband in the home. My mother probably did not feel like it then, but she was a strong woman. Like most women in matriarchal families, she "held it down," doing all she knew how to do, raising me and my two sisters.

Of all the mistakes and shortcomings of my parents, the amazing truth was that my mom was sober, and she was saved! What a miracle on multiple fronts. Addiction ran generations deep in my family, on both sides. And that path of life came for me with a vengeance.

Going to church week after week taught a young Christian mother one thing. My mother learned to pray. I believe her prayers speak to this day into the souls of countless children and many more to come.

In those early years, mom began to pray for me and my sisters. No matter how she felt, no matter how ominous it looked, she held onto the hem of His garment, and she was not going to let go until He blessed her children. I remember I would come home in the early hours of the morning after being out drinking and partying, and there she would be—sitting in her chair with an open Bible on her lap, weeping and crying out to the Lord on our behalf.

When we were real young, on the way to school, our mother would quote Psalm 91. But we were typical bratty kids. We would just roll our eyes and say, "There goes mom again." She stood on scripture. I heard her repeat countless times. Now I know it's Isaiah 54:13. She would recite: "I will teach my *daughters* of the Lord, and the well-being of my *daughters* shall be great." I don't know if she understood, at that time, the power there is in words. And when those words are God's words, they hold the creative ability to prophecy a new future, regardless of the present condition. She was a woman of faith.

My dad would have wild parties at our house, sometimes lasting for days. Even so, my mom would "drag" us to church on Sunday morning. Talk about confusing!

I remember one time when mom was at her wit's end with my father, his brothers, and their friend's parties, drunken conversations, and even people hallucinating from a "bad" high. She wanted to scream! She would go into the garage and pick up the phone and call TBN or other Christian prayer warriors and ask someone, anyone on the other end, to please pray with her. And they did.

Growing up in such a conflicting environment gave me a skewed perspective of God, to say the least. My opinion then was that God was powerless. Of course, He is not, but that was how my young mind understood Him to be. I said to myself, "If this is your God, I don't want Him." I saw my dad having what appeared to be fun, so without hesitation, I chose his lifestyle.

While I had accepted Jesus in my heart at VBS as a child of about six years of age, I had consciously turned my back on Him by the age of thirteen. After my father left home when I was eleven, I began the journey that so many youths take. His absence created a hearts' cry and question: What do I do with this massive, gaping hole in my heart? Am I not worthy of His love? Was I not important or valuable enough for Him to stay? So, I did what the generation before me did and the generation before them. I went searching for love in all the wrong places. I don't know if we as a society understand the importance of the father's role in the life of their children. My dad was not physically or verbally abusive. All he had to do was walk out and not come back. That was enough to send me down the slippery slope of confusion, fear, lack of identity, and damaged self-esteem.

I was a rebellious, angry, confused, wounded young girl who was pretty sure God was: a) powerless, b) mad, and c) wouldn't want someone like me. For the next ten years, I paid dearly for that decision, which I will discuss at length in a later chapter. I was a wide-open target for the enemy of my soul, and he had his way with me. I was totally powerless against his tactics and completely ignorant of his devices.

At just sixteen, I became a mother. By eighteen, I was an alcoholic. At nineteen, I was introduced to methamphetamines. Encountering domestic violence was particularly tragic. There is nothing like physical abuse to instill the message and drive the point home: You are worthless, you have no value, *not* even God could love you.

By nineteen, I had given birth to my second son, whom I had to walk through the very painful steps of giving up for adoption. And at just twenty years old, choosing to have an abortion was the result of my lifestyle and its consequences. Hopelessness, despair, and failure were all I considered for my life to amount to.

Addiction was how I coped. Abuse, rejection, and abandonment were constant companions. This mindset was driven down deep into my soul and the souls of many Native American people. The truth is, these types of problems and others plague many *people* everywhere!

Concluding Reflections

I will continue with my story in a later chapter. But for now, concerning our reservations across America, many people want to know: "What are the root issues or causes of these problems—alcoholism, drugs, spousal abuse, incarceration, children removed from their homes? Others? Can these atrocities really be happening right in my own nation?" These are important questions to ask. A genuine desire to be educated is a positive start towards healing and change.

Government-funded programs, rehab centers, and "do-good" non-profits are good but only a temporary fix. Truth is, surface level, band-aid efforts cannot heal spirit-level wounds.

To educate or bring awareness concerning the enemy's tactics against the First Nations people, there are two lenses that I would like us to consider in the next couple of chapters.

Imagine having a pair of glasses. Obviously, you would have two lenses. If there were two subjects that I could put on these lenses and whoever wore them would understand and have clearer vision and insight, I would choose the lenses of:

1. The reality of the spirit realm, and
2. some events in America's history.

Without such background, the result is an inability to focus clearly. Understanding is darkened, affecting beliefs, behaviors, and responses.

First, let's look at some often overlooked but key historical events and the enemies' desire to deceive from the beginning of time.

3

American History, Children and the Misrepresentation of God

◄————————►)●(◄————————►

"Now the serpent was more cunning
than any beast of the field which the
Lord God had made..."

~Genesis 3:1a (NKJV)~

We must be educated regarding the past, *but not to open old wounds and reinforce the pain.* No! To me, one thing that is more alarming than the facts that surround America's history as it pertains to First Nations people is the fact that so few have any awareness about it. The purpose of talking about our past is to better understand our present and begin to look forward to a powerful future.

Abuse of Political Power and Historical Trauma

Today, one can easily research and find YouTube documentaries, dedicated websites, as well as books, and much information on the subject of the historical trauma the first peoples of America faced. Unfortunately, one place you will rarely if ever, find this information is in the public school system, or more specifically, in a class on US history.

Seizing 1.5 Billion Acres of Land

Between 1776 and 1887, the United States government seized over 1.5 billion acres of land from America's indigenous people through treaties and executive orders. The YouTube video "The Invasion of America"[3] shows how this land cessation happened by mapping every treaty and executive order during that time period. It concludes with a map of present-day federally recognized Indian reservations.

The following is a paraphrase of an article by Claudio Saunt, the Associate Director of the Institute of Native American Studies at the University of Georgia.

Since most lands were "ceded" using treaties, it may appear that Native Americans gave up their land willingly and peacefully, but in many cases, they had no other options and handed over the land through bribery or force. The Government also used federal legislation and executive order to take land from natives. In the 19th century, Presidents like Andrew Jackson, Abraham Lincoln, and Grover Cleveland created small reservations for tribes that once controlled vast areas. *The Invasion of America* is a stark demonstration of how quickly these legal fictions were used to erase people

and just how much what was once their
land we now claim as our own.

Just one example of this is the Black Hills of South
Dakota, the He' Sapa. These were sacred lands populated
and owned by the Lakota Sioux. Not only were these and
surrounding lands taken, but it was also done through fierce
violence, murder, and greed, resulting in what is now known
as "The Wounded Knee Massacre" of 1890. There is a book
written by Dee Brown in 1970 that I highly recommend—
Bury My Heart at Wounded Knee. Brown documents the sys-
tematic destruction of the American Indian during the second half of the nineteenth century. The book was later made
into a movie in 2007.

Nothing could possibly be more offensive than to take
ownership of these sacred mountains from their original
inhabitants, right? Think again. Modern-day Mt. Rushmore
attracts millions of tourists each year. The United States
President's faces chiseled into the side of the massive rock is
both majestic and awe-inspiring to behold, for sure. What is
not widely divulged, however, is that in doing so, to Natives,
it has been considered a desecration of what was once their
own. Even so, to this day, this man-made, seven-wonders-
of-the-world shrine stands tall and proud. As a celebratory
landmark to the European settlers, it seems to serve as an
ominous and continual reminder to the host people of the
region regarding injustice and historical wrongs at the hands
of government, greed, and power. (see Photo #6 on page
242)

Sadly, even to this day, many non-natives hold a skewed
perspective of Native American history, one often rooted in
fear. Some people have what I call a "border-town mentality."
Living so close to the overwhelming issues, they often adopt

an accusatory stance. Such a mentality is cold and prideful. Seemingly to stand high and look down low as if to say, "Why don't they just get over it?" And this solution is often offered without a true understanding of what "it" is.

Some, however, just plain feel the weight of inadequacy and helplessness to do anything about the incredibly difficult problems surrounding our reservations. Also, we all fail to realize the corruption and decay in our own hearts and communities. It simply manifests itself in different statistical forms.

What I provide in this chapter is nowhere near all-inclusive. So, please take what you hear and conduct your own research.

The story of Native American children today is not told in its fullness without first looking back in time. For the purpose of this book and for raising the awareness of Native American children today, there is simply no way around this chapter in history.

Seizing Native American Children

The Indian Child Welfare Act (ICWA) was enacted in 1978. Prior to the enactment, the Indian Adoption Project of 1958 (lasting to 1967) allowed government officials to remove American Indian children from their parents and tribal communities to be adopted by white families. In other words, it was legal. The intent of the Indian Adoption Act was to assimilate native children. This assimilation strategy stole their cultural identity and connection to their tribal government.

The story of the Native American people is complicated and marked by significant trauma and atrocities, which resulted in the largest genocide of the 19th Century. Efforts to assimilate Indians into mainstream American society often involved the *removal of native children from their homes* on tribal land and sending them to religious and BIA (Bureau of Indian Affairs) boarding schools. Fueled by Richard Henry Pratt's belief that Indians could be "civilized" through total immersion, these schools prohibited children from speaking their language, following their cultural practices, or spiritual beliefs. What happened to these young vulnerable children in many of these schools resulted in overwhelming, long-standing effects of trauma and unresolved grief. These traumas, which interrupted the ability to parent, have led to most of the current social problems which plague Indian communities today.[4]

"I am a red man. If the Great Spirit had desired me to be a white man.
He would have made me so in the first place. God made me an Indian."

~Chief Sitting Bull~

American Indian Boarding Schools

The actual agenda of the Indian boarding schools was that of ethnic cleansing. General Richard Pratt, the founder of Carlisle Indian Industrial Boarding School and a champion of assimilation, summarized his vision this way: "Kill the Indian. Save the man." Quite literally, it was genocide disguised by education. Adding even deeper insult to injury, harsh punishment, and abuse of all kinds (sexual, physical, mental, emotional, and spiritual) towards children became part of the story.[5]

The trauma of removing a generation of children from their homes and "colonizing" them into a way of life that was separate from the Creator's original intent has caused generational effects that cut deep and wide. This loss of identity, language, and cultural integrity has created cycles of the disintegration of the family, resulting in extreme despair and, in many cases, extreme addiction.

Many of today's mothers and fathers are simply perpetuating the pain that has been passed down to them. What happens when we get snared by the web of sins against our mothers and fathers? We end up carrying yesterday's wounds deep within our souls today, and they bleed into tomorrow's generation. We end up with cycles of bondage passed down and reinforced through entrenched mindsets. The resulting implications wreak havoc upon the lives of children today who are in constant jeopardy of alcoholism, drugs, domestic violence, and parental incarceration. These cycles will perpetuate *until someone rises up to stop them.*

With a long history of greed, injustice, and systems of assimilation, sometimes all in the name of God, a long history of unforgiveness, resentment and animosity naturally follow. Big doses of *distrust* for the US Government, its programs, and also Christianity, or more specifically, organized religion, remain an issue to this day. There is a deeply ruptured foundation causing a serious stigma attached to "Foster Care," "Group Homes," Christian, or "religious" ministries, and missionaries. Though improving, it is still alive and well.

Tragically, the damage that has been done to indigenous people groups by the hands of those claiming to represent Jesus or Christianity has driven a generational wedge between them and the One True God, resulting in such perceptions as "Jesus is the white man's God."

I would love to recommend a book called "Whiteman's Gospel," written by Craig Stephen Smith, a Chippewa from the Leech Lake Reservation of Minnesota. He makes a couple of powerful points that really stuck out to me, such as his comparison of Israel and Native peoples. I simply must place an excerpt here, as it speaks well to this topic.

> *"Indian people have had contact with Christianity basically only for the past few hundred years…Redemption through Jesus Christ has been in existence for nearly two thousand years. Most of the contact Indian people have had with the messengers of this message has been basically the white, Anglo-Saxon people from Europe. For that reason, and that reason alone, Indian people have equated Christianity with the white man, and hence, the concept developed that it's the Whiteman's Gospel.*
>
> *The realization that God chose [Israel]—a minority, tribal group of people to bring salvation to the world and reconciliation between God and His creation is not normally the way Native people view Christianity. But this is the truth."*

Honestly, I struggle with using the word "missionary" at all. The concept of a Christian missionary insinuates the idea of being a Christ-follower. The counterfeit misrepresentation of Christ (obviously not by all Christian or "religious" missionaries, but you get my point) has created deeply engrained wounds leading to negative mindsets over many (obviously not all) First Nations people, and understandably so. *If Jesus is misrepresented, naturally, He will be rejected.*

Excerpt taken from:
***Rescuing the Gospel from the Cowboys** By Richard Twiss*

In 2012, I sat with some friends and acquaintances for their weekly luncheon discussion. They were all white Christian businessmen. We had been discussing "white privilege" for a few weeks, and I had been sharing a bit about bad missions theology, genocide, boarding schools and the devastating effect of colonization in our communities. A gentleman I have known for several years, a highly successful businessman and supporter of missionary work in Mexico, said, "Well, Richard, don't you think it's better for your people that we, a Christian democracy, conquered your people? After all, it could have been the Nazis, Russians or Japanese. Somebody was going to eventually conquer you, so don't you think your people are better off that it was us rather than someone else?"

I was angry, and these words came like a flood. I clearly, carefully and precisely said, "So let me get this straight. Are you saying we should be grateful that your people came here and brutally sodomized us? Are you saying we are better off for being sodomized by you and we should be grateful for it? And we should be glad that you used the Bible as a lubricant to brutally sodomize us? Is this what you are saying to me?" After a few moments of dead silence in the room, I then said, "The vulgarity of my words pales in comparison to the vulgarity of your words." The images I saw when I said those words had, as a backdrop, pregnant Native women being cut open and their babies' heads smashed with rifle butts; entire villages of old men, women and children being bludgeoned to death after the women were defiled in the worst imaginable ways; forced starvation, violent imprisonment and torture; tens of thousands of little Indian boys and girls being hauled off to boarding schools where they were plagued with sexual, physical and psychological abuse of immeasurable cruelty and enduring devastation. The gross inhumanity that crushed our people was of the most horrific and vulgar in Western History.

The missionary views the world, including the people he or she walks among, through a set of deeply embedded, culturally conditioned lenses or realities, both at a conscious and subconscious level. Starting with the missionaries who arrived to work among the Eastern tribes in the 1600s through the present, this has not changed.

Sadly, many missionaries from the past couldn't see the people they were sent to serve as fellow children of Creator, created in his image and precious in his sight. Their perception was obscured by their worldview.

In my first fourteen years of embracing Jesus, I conformed to the expectation to accept interpretations of the Bible that said "old things had passed away and all things had become white."

Source: Twiss, *Rescuing the Gospel from the Cowboys*, 62-63, 69, 82.

Deception by Slander

The misrepresentation of Creator did not begin with the cowboys and Indians, however. The misrepresentation of Creator is linked all the way back to "the beginning" in the garden with Eve.

The Bible records the very first transgression being deception through slander. "Slander" is defined as damaging someone's character or reputation, defaming by misrepresenting, or causing someone to have a bad opinion of another.

We know that Satan, as a serpent, came to Eve in order to get her to *question God's reputation*. The serpents' game plan? To plant questions, concerning God, in her mind that she might reach a false conclusion.

When Eve was presented with the opportunity to eat the fruit, the enemy told her, "You will not surely die." The serpent suggested the idea that God is not who He says He is. He says one thing, but He means another. He is unreliable. Satan's comments introduced doubt and suspicion towards God's character and reputation, climaxing with Eve eating the forbidden fruit. The power of slander denied Eve her proximity or connection with God.

How did the enemy get Eve to reject God's goodness and commit this act of disobedience, thereby causing a separation between Eve and her Creator, and between Creator and *every* generation since?

The role of the serpent found in Genesis 3:1 provides an answer. "Now the serpent was more cunning than any beast of the field which the Lord God had made. And he said to the woman, "Has God indeed said…" The etymology of the word "serpent" in this verse is *nachash,* which means: To practice divination and enchantment; to hiss which means to whisper a magic spell as a soothsayer; to use sorcery or witchcraft. What was happening to Eve while she was listening to the words of the tempter? It is just as if she were being placed underneath a spell.

In fact, this Greek word for sorcery here is *pharmakeia,* meaning the use of administering drugs to cause an altered state of consciousness in order to manipulate and control. *Pharmakeia* is where we get our English word for pharmacy. A deeper meaning than today's understanding of pharmacy is to literally mean: *One who prepares or uses magical remedies in order to put under the influence.* Truly, all humanity has fallen underneath the intoxicating hiss of the deceivers lies, linked back to the very beginning of time. The result is a catastrophic disconnect from the Source of all life.

Satan was the first to misrepresent God and His character, and there have been countless falsifications and misinterpretations since. These spell-binding concoctions have successfully lured man away from his loving Father for generations.

Genesis 3:8 (BRG) states, "They [Adam and Eve] heard the voice of the Lord God walking in the Garden in the cool of the day; and Adam and his wife *hid from the presence of the Lord* God." Today, there is such suffering and yearning for reconnection to Truth and life. The earth is literally groaning in moral decay and under the weight of being disconnected from our original atmosphere of glory in the Garden. We were created to live in connection with and proximity to Creator, who is life (Psalm 91).

> "If something is removed from
> its natural environment
> you don't have to actively kill it;
> it will die on its own."
>
> ~ Apostle Guillermo Maldonado ~

Anywhere there is abuse of human beings, domination, manipulation, control, and religious practices that are counter-Bible or Antichrist, what you are observing are the effects of spiritual warfare or spell-binding sorcery, as it was through the serpent towards Eve. People involved in such practices are themselves underneath this demonic influence. As a result, they are knowingly or unknowingly co-laboring with the prince of this world, whose master agenda is to defame Jesus Christ so people will shun Him.

The Bible is clear that there is only One Way that reconnects us to Creator, and that is specifically through His Son, Jesus Christ. Jesus says of Himself in John 14:6 (ERV): "I Am the way, the truth, and the life. The only way to the Father is through Me." Jesus is the only way whereby people can be saved (Acts 4:12). He is the One who heals, delivers, and sets free (John 8:36). He is the absolute source of all life (John 1:1-5).

If so, then the devil himself would somehow need to successfully turn, in this case, First Nations people, but in reality—all people, any people—in the opposite direction from that Truth that sets all free. In this light, Satan's strategy to camouflage himself behind "so-called Christianity" in order to defame Jesus' reputation *amongst the First Nations people* makes perfect sense.

This disconnect, of course, only results in generational devastation and harm. Satan loves for trauma, pain, and the deep wounds of the soul to be passed down from one generation to the next. This is how he gains "legal" access into that individual, family, or nation. Those experiencing the abuse or injustice are now in danger of being put underneath the same demonic spell but in the form of unforgiveness and bitterness of the soul. Such inner disruption casts a long, dark shadow upon the human soul, resulting in deep wounds.

What Wounds the Human Soul?

We are created in the image and likeness of God Himself. He desires to live inside us so that we can reflect His mind, heart, compassion, love, and on and on.

When the human soul is *separated* from Creator, it inflicts a deep wound. Think of a simple illustration of two pieces of paper glued together. Once dried, any attempt to pull the two pieces apart becomes impossible, at least not without ripping or tearing the paper and making a big mess. This analogy serves as a picture that describes the condition of the soul of humanity.

Wounds on the soul effect:

- the *mind,* resulting in toxic, tormenting chatter and disturbing thoughts, creating damaging belief patterns.
- the *emotions,* resulting in overwhelmingly painful, negative, and hurtful reactions, such as feelings of deep sorrow, sadness, fear, anxiety, depression, and even torment.
- the *will,* resulting in ungodly and unbeneficial decisions. Even when you "know better," you tend to make choices that hurt yourself and others because of a vexed soul.

These wounds remain until the human soul receives healing, which can only be found in Creator God through His Son Jesus Christ (Acts 4:12). Although salvation is received instantly and the spirit of a person is recreated in a moment, the soul has to be healed over a process of time and renewed daily.

Just ask yourself—how can a mother leave her child and never come back? How can someone go through with an abortion? How can someone beat on another human being seemingly with no conscience? How does such evil perpetuate? Separation from the source of life and light results in death and darkness in its many forms.

The Wounds of a Nation

What do you do when the soul of an entire people group has undergone extreme levels of societal trauma and has, in effect, become deeply wounded? What do you do when the enemy comes as an angel of light to misrepresent and slander Creator God? All too often, negative or destructive strongholds of thought, feeling, and their corresponding actions become accepted as mainstream. A belief system that concludes "this is just how it is" pervades, like a familiar blanket. When this happens, a person, place, or region can end up with portals of darkness that can be deep and expansive, resulting in the harsh, cold statistics that follow.

Concluding Reflections

There has been some serious damage inflicted, through Historical trauma and religion.

Those who are called to meet the needs of those affected must have some understanding of the spirit world and how it operates. Why? Because everything happens in the spirit world first and then manifests in the physical world.

I will share in more detail how my battles with the spirit world manifested in my own life in a later chapter. But for now, we must look behind the scenes for an overview of the very real, unseen spirit world in the next two chapters.

4

The Invisible Spirit-World

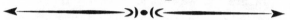

"For we wrestle not against flesh and
blood, but against *principalities*,
against *powers*, against the *rulers of the darkness of this world*,
against *spiritual wickedness* in high places."

~Ephesians 6:12 (KJV)~

"This world is just a shadow of the spirit world."

~Chief Crazy Horse~

The greatest trick the devil ever pulled was convincing the world that he doesn't exist. If we don't fall for that, his next move is to make us believe that if we ignore him, he will go away or leave us alone.

One quick glance around us today, and it's clear that the Body of Christ must *awaken and arise* in this hour to our God-given authority in the earth. This is the battle. Yes! There is a battle, and yes, you are called to it in some way, shape, or form. This battle is not personal. It is familial, generational, regional, and global. This is our enemies' laser-focus: keep the believer from understanding, much less actively engaged and operating from, the finished work of the Cross.

Spiritual blindness, comfortability, and self-focus seem to be the crux of warfare, not just over the world but also over the American church. The arrows of passivity and near-sightedness are being heaved relentlessly in our direction. I pray these words will jolt and jar us into reality! Spirit-world reality! And let it begin with me, Lord.

As advocates and ambassadors of heaven, we must always remember as we engage in a cause that demands justice, we are fighting the spirit(s) behind the evil, not the person or persons promoting it. Why? Because the Bible says we are not to be *ignorant* of Satan's devices (evil schemes, intentions, and ponderings), lest he secures an advantage over us (2 Corinthians 2:11). The word *ignorant* in this verse simply means to not know or understand, to err. How easily we can do this when stepping out into our assignments.

People can sometimes experience a *backlash* from the enemy when they fail to understand or operate according to the knowledge that is settled in transcendent truth. God said this about his chosen, "My people are destroyed for lack of knowledge." Note His people were destroyed *not* for lack of anointing or finances or love, *but for lack of knowledge.* Lord grant us wisdom as we advance.

A Basic Biblical Understanding of the Spirit Realm

In order to confront evil, we must make up our minds to *never* lose sight of the real enemy; rather, we must focus intently on Jesus. When you know your enemy, you will be able to connect the punches. Instead of fighting in the flesh and beating at the air, we must follow Paul's example: "Therefore I do not run without a definite goal; I do not flail around like one beating the air [shadow boxing]" (1 Corinthians 9:26, Amplified Bible).

This chapter is in no way an exhaustive study of the basic biblical understanding of the spirit realm. There are many books on this subject available for further study. Rather, I offer a basic overview here as it is vitally important for us to have an understanding.

Operations Behind Evil Activity

Ephesians 6 clearly defines the hierarchy in the spirit world who have assignments over and against the whole earth. Specifically, verses 10-12 admonish us to be strong in the Lord and in the power of His might: "Put on the whole armor of God, that you may be able *to stand against the wiles* of the devil. For we *wrestle* not against flesh and blood, but against *principalities*, against *powers*, against *rulers of the darkness* of this world, against *spiritual hosts of wickedness* in heavenly places."

Our battle is *not* against people. It's *not* against your spouse, the grocery store clerk, or your co-worker. It's *not* against the Church. It's *not* against the Government. Our battle is *not* even our prejudices, drugs, or violence because every evil activity is *inspired by an evil spirit.* Our battle *is* about Satan and his cohorts! We are spiritual enforcers.

The purpose of this "armor" is to enable the believer to *stand against the wiles* of the devil. The Greek word for *wiles* is *"methodeia"* from where we get the English word "methods" or "mode of operations." *Wiles* refers to strategies, schemes, and tricks. The word *wrestle* in this verse is the Greek word *"pale,"* which literally means a battle in which each endeavor to overthrow the other, where victory is achieved when the antagonist is laid out prostrate, being held down by the opponent's hand upon the neck.

The Bible confirms that the devil is a defeated foe! Jesus won a complete victory over Satan, hell, and the grave! We are *not* powerless victims to the sabotaging strategies of hell. Our authority in the finished work of Christ is *not* in question. What is in question? *Our knowledge and understanding of our authority in Christ and His finished work and our ability to skillfully enforce that authority.*

The Kingdom of Darkness is Structured

Allow me to break down the meaning of some of these words from Ephesians 6:12 in Greek.

a. "principalities" is *arche,* which means the leader; that by which anything originates, the beginning or origin. Principalities are the highest-ranking, ruling spirits operating in designated jurisdictions.

b. "powers" is *exousia,* which means, in this context, the enemy's ability or might to hold one submissive to his will in order to subdue, drive out and destroy.

c. "rulers" is *kosmokrator,* which refers to the god of this world (2 Corinthians 4:4), the prince of this age, the devil, and his demons. Rulers of darkness empower people (because of their depravity of light) to commit heinous crimes.

d. "wickedness" is *pomeria,* which means evil, unclean, proud, lying, deceitful, malicious.

These spiritual entities rule the world. They are darkness dominators who hold sway over people who are ignorant of divine things. This evil posse headquarters in the second heaven or aerial heavens, above us, but inferior to God. They are calculating our every weakness as they desire to govern our thoughts, words, and actions.

Jezebel, Death, and Antichrist

Three examples of Ephesians 6:12 chief darkness dominators would be the spirit of Jezebel, the spirit of Death, and the spirit of Antichrist.

Jezebel:	Manipulation and control, sexual perversion, strife, rebellion and deception
Death:	Ailments, spirits of infirmity, pre-mature death, generational curses, destruction, war; suicide, abortion, hatred, spiritual death; spirits that subdue, conquer, and defeat.
Antichrist/Religion:	Scripture speaks of a physical Antichrist that will appear one day (Revelation, 13). Until then, realize the spirit of Antichrist is already in the land, operating in the form of anything that opposes or is against the anointing.

For example, false religions that are bewitching segments of culture, such as evolution, atheism, humanism, etc., are steeped in our American education system. Indoctrinating a unified stand against a genuine move of God is another definition of the Antichrist spirit.

When looking at the following statistics, it becomes easier to see from where (in the spirit world) these are coming from:

- Certain sicknesses or diseases, such as diabetes, cancer, and even premature death, are prevalent.
- A high rate of domestic violence, murder, or incarceration.
- Accepted prejudice or hatred prevail in certain geographical regions.
- Child sexual abuse, incest, molestation, or child sex crimes are prevalent.
- Extreme poverty is considered "just the way it is" in some areas; and
- The selling and use of methamphetamines are extremely high in certain regions.

Literally, the list of the statistics, as well as the spirits behind it in the unseen realm, are endless. And fortunately, we do not need to have a complete list, total understanding, or Doctorate in Theology and demonology, etc. However, to deny spirit-world-activity is to be ignorant of Satan's devices (2 Corinthians 2:11). Meaning, even if we close our eyes, it still exists. The spirits behind the statistics desire to remain hidden, that they may continue and perpetuate evil.

Our society wants answers. Our world wants to solve and alleviate the ills of human suffering. However, we want to do it without involving God. We cannot choose to live outside the confines of our Creator's instructions and expect things to work well.

First John 3:8 records the very reason Jesus was sent: "For this purpose was the Son of God manifested that He might destroy the works of the devil." This is literally why

He came. To demolish the enemy's strategies and dissolve the kingdom of darkness.

When we allow scriptural truth to "open the eyes of our understanding" to these realities, we can begin to shift our focus from merely what we see with our natural eyes and respond to wage *good warfare* (1 Timothy 1:18). Why is it good warfare? Because our victory, through Jesus' blood, is secured!

Territorial Dominion

Territorial spirits cause the pervasive culture or atmosphere. They are unleashed across the whole earth and simply manifest their evils differently in each specific geographical area and its' people.

Eventually, those living in the territories begin to identify with things that are counter-truth, accepting and assigning such behaviors as community norms. With each passing generation, they are further strengthened and solidified, creating deeply embedded mindsets, philosophies, strongholds, and belief systems (Deuteronomy 5:9).

Harsh statistics over a region relate to the blatant "problems" in a particular place where societal or cultural "norms" of ungodliness, immorality, and evil are operating in plain sight for all to see. These evils are caused by territorial dominators in the unseen and result in the devastation and degradation of individuals, families, and communities.

There is a battle in the heavenlies that affects every aspect of our lives. Again, there is absolutely no comparison between God and Satan. Satan and God are not equal. God overpowers Satan exponentially and has won a complete victory through the life, death, resurrection, and ascension of Jesus Christ, and there is no contest. However, Satan is not fighting God. Satan is opposing Gods' people and God's kingdom plans. This is the "wrestle."

Even when territorial spirits are recognized and rightfully linked to the corresponding cold realities, oftentimes, they are left unchallenged because they are seemingly too vast in size and strength, too powerful to contest. The root issues and ancient access points into a person, people, or nation are entrenched in generations of pain, pride, and trauma.

Legal Access Points

The enemy must be given permission or granted legal access to enter a person or place. He stealthily, systematically, and relentlessly looks for doorways, or access points, in order to devour (1 Peter 5:8). Doorways for access include such things as:

- deception and disobedience, resulting in *sin*—whether our own sin or sins committed against us;
- *generational sin and iniquity* passed down through the bloodline (bloodline curses);
- the *wounded*, traumatized soul marked by *unforgiveness*, bitterness, resentment, hatred, pride, or rebellion;
- *ignorance* (lack of revelation and light).

In fact, the dark spirit world is just looking for souls, wounded by any of the above and more, and the open door it provides.

After successful entry, the adversary's cohorts can quickly infiltrate an area. Using a whole arsenal of strategies and schemes, they flood and overwhelm, thereby establishing residency and claiming territory.

The DNA of an individual does not only determine physical attributes, such as the color of hair, skin, or eyes but also carries the characteristics of the soul (mental, emotional, and behavioral).

Concerning Native American Children, Youth, and Families

My focus is on Native American regions explicitly. As we ponder the plight of our children, it is obvious something is wrong:

> Child Abuse and Neglect: A report of child abuse is made every ten seconds. At least five children die every day from child abuse (National Clinical Assessment Service). Domestic Violence: Three-fourths of Native American women have experienced some type of sexual assault (American Indian Women's Chemical Health Project).
>
> Child Sexual Abuse: One of the most destructive problems affecting children in Indian Country today is sexual abuse (molestation and rape).
>
> Other Issues: Young Native Americans today live their lives surrounded with and immersed in poverty, hopelessness, and despair, and suicide.

> Drugs and Alcoholism in the Native American community are epidemic. More tribal youth die from alcohol than from any other drug (The Indian Reporter).

The drug called meth (methamphetamines), for example, plagues our reservations today. This particular drug has certain spirits attached to it, namely the spirits of homicide, suicide, murder, and death. Like the spirit of alcoholism, this drug also carries with it the ability to incapacitate moms and dads to the degree that they give up their children in the name of their addiction.

To whom do parents give away their children? It seems natural to answer, "the foster care system." But the reason behind this answer is not natural. In reality, there is a spiritual-rooted reason why our children in mass numbers are "being given up." The spirit behind meth (requires your children to be separated from you). Thankfully, there are many very good Foster Care and Group Homes that are kingdom-minded, ministering the true Gospel of Jesus Christ and His love. But we all know that all too often, tragedies happen in some foster and group homes, not unlike what happened in the homes from which they were removed, or sometimes worse.

This *generation* of children and youth are being offered up to *something*. Even if children are not literally and physically sacrificed, there is a serious sacrifice of the quality of life. A simple glance at the hardship and conditions our young people face, and it becomes obvious there is something operating "behind the scenes."

These ailments, problems, and crises, along with their negative outcomes, are not just coming from nowhere.

Dominating principalities and powers are unleashed into their assigned territories to operate and perpetuate evil through fallen humanity.

The enemy can easily masquerade behind political correctness, government, humanistic educational systems, and false religions. The fear of confronting perpetrators or offending victims who are already wounded can also be a deterrent. This is exactly what the enemy wants—to remain undetected. If he can keep us confused and fighting about the consequences of our sin, then the root cause remains hidden and undisturbed, allowing him the freedom to operate at will.

Remember, whatever issues we see manifested in our regions in the natural have a demonic reality governing from the spiritual.

Let's look at a few examples of contact points between the seen and unseen in this next chapter.

5

High Places

◄────────►)●(◄────────►

"But you are a chosen generation, a royal priesthood,
a holy nation, His own special people,
that you may proclaim the praises of
Him who called you out
of darkness into His marvelous light."

~1 Peter 2:9 (NKJV)~

Remember the game when you were a kid, King of the Mountain? Also known as King of the Hill or King of the Castle, it was a children's game when I was growing up. The object of which is to stay on top of a large hill or pile (or any other designated area), "no matter what." Whoever did was considered "King of the Mountain."

You would have to be tough. You had to fight for that position and title, forcefully pushing back all the other kids running to the top, securing your moment of rulership! At least until the school bell rang, and it was time for lunch. Surely there were always those one or two crazy kids who would end up fist-fighting or wrestling for the coveted position. Not me. All someone had to do was look at me crazy, and I would retreat. I was never really "queen of the hill," I guess you could say. I didn't want to fight, hurt, or offend anyone, so I would simply concede.

The truth is there is a war in the spirit realm for the high places throughout the regions of the world. At (spiritual) high places, rulership is determined. It is where altars of worship are erected and serviced that consequently "push back" the opposition and "win" the territory.

However, in this case, it is no game.

Altar Worship

What is an altar? An altar is a sacred place of prayer or worship to God or gods. Altars are a contact place with the invisible spirit world, providing gateways or portals, where business in the spiritual realm is conducted. At altars, blessing (for good) or cursing (for evil) are transmitted from the spirit realm into the earth, ultimately creating the spiritual culture or atmosphere we live in.

Altars are a place of sacrifices, spiritual transactions, and the making of covenants. Again, for good or evil. From the days of the Old Testament until now, covenants and altars require blood sacrifice.

First Peter 2:9 says we are a new testament royal priesthood. The duty of the priesthood, the people of God, is to tend the altars of prayer, worship, and spiritual dominion in our assigned jurisdictions. I wonder if that's why it can seem so difficult to pray, to study the word, to give a sacrifice of praise and worship? Not because these are insignificant disciplines, but because they are what's required from the people of God in order to maintain the spiritual authority and atmospheres in dark, dark places.

The reason we even have the privilege to be a new testament priesthood is because the King of Kings poured out His blood on a hill called Golgotha.

In fact, each time we come to God in prayer, we are not coming on our own authority. We are coming covered in the blood of Jesus. The Bible says it is because of His blood that we are able to "draw near with a true heart" (Hebrews 10:19, 22).

The kingdom of darkness is a counterfeit to God's kingdom. The enemy is not a creator, he is a fraud. Remember, he fell like lightning from heaven (Luke 10:19) because of pride. He lost his position, his relationship with God, and his authority, and that is exactly what he wants for you and me.

We were created to worship God and to walk in fellowship, co-laboring in the earth, empowered by His Spirit. The foundation of Satan's kingdom is faulty, being deception. Deception intercepts the light and lures the heart of man, seducing us into accepting his fate as our own.

Altars Require Bloodshed

First Kings 11:1-10 discusses King Solomon, whose heart was beginning to be drawn away from Yahweh because of the many wives he took. Verse 7 reveals an outward demonstration of Solomon's inward heart condition when he "built a high place" for his wives' pagan gods of Baal, Ashtoreth, Chemosh, and Milcom (11:5). One common theme throughout the worship practices to these deities was child sacrifice. Yes, child sacrifice. And such persists today!

Many people understand that satanic activity, not unlike that found in the Old Testament, is alive and well in this generation. No one in their right mind would be accepting of babies being slaughtered at altars for ceremonial worship, except Satan worshippers, obviously.

However, at its root, abortion is a form of modern-day altar worship, where blood is being perpetually offered. As grievous as abortion is to Creator, the giver and sustainer of all life, it exists and perpetuates, basically at will, *because it hides* behind the veil of "political correctness." Ever hear these comments? "You don't know what that mom is facing," or "You don't know the details surrounding the situation, so don't judge."

Again, for the purpose of this chapter, I use abortion as an example to highlight the root cause and effect *behind the act,* not of the precious women who have fallen prey to these realities. For all of us, myself included, who have participated in an abortion, the truth is that the *blood of Jesus* can and will forgive any and every sin we have ever committed when we turn to Him in repentance. That includes having an abortion. I know because I am forgiven. His grace is truly amazing!

But just like the frog in the kettle analogy, when it becomes too late to jump out, we as a society can become desensitized and then blinded to the evil spiritual roots; it becomes an accepted norm. Regardless of society's acceptance, with each baby whose life is snuffed out, and in America, that is approximately 22 percent of all pregnancies, the principalities are being appeased and thereby increasing in strength and power, or rulership.

This is one example of spiritual realm activity lurking behind the scenes.

Tradition and Religion

Another example of blood on altars is some ceremonial practices that are observed to this day. Some traditions require the piercing of flesh, causing blood to flow. However, whether bloodshed is required or not, any form of worship that is in the name of anything or anyone other than in the Name of Creator's Son, Jesus, opens up doors of legal entrance for the enemy. Are some, obviously not all, traditions, practices, and forms of worship doing just that?

This subject is a tricky one because the dark side can and will *hide* behind many beautiful parts. God-created cultures, in and of themselves, have much beauty to offer. The incredible, God-given uniqueness of all people is awe-inspiring and demanding of honor, respect, and allegiance.

Our enemy has a very real, three-part agenda for the nations of the world: *steal, kill, destroy* (John 10:10). He won't necessarily be able to accomplish such a lofty goal if we were able to "see" his strategies for what they really are. Scripture says that Satan comes *disguised* as an angel of light (2 Corinthians 11:14). This strategy is genius because to be disguised means: having changed one's appearance in order to conceal one's identity. He has certainly transformed and masqueraded himself to us all at some point, and probably in some way, currently.

Any observed religion and forms of worship, where Christ is not central, is demonic in origin, and deliberate deception is at work. Period. This is true of any and *all* forms of religion or worship, regardless of how beautiful or "filled with light" or "harmless it appears" or how deep-seated in custom and practice.

The truth is Joseph Smith is not King of Kings. Neither is White Buffalo Calf Woman, Charles Taze Russell, Muhamad, or David Spangler.

Like my previous example, exposing truth can be difficult because the principalities in the invisible world do not want to be confronted. Some forms of worship and religious belief systems are rooted in idolatry. The Bible is clear in Exodus 20:3: "You shall have no other gods before Me." Verse 5 goes on to say the iniquity of the fathers *passes on to the children* to the third and fourth generation.

When any form of worship, where Jesus Christ is not central, even if passed down for many generations, the form of worship itself can become an idol and an identity. If this is the case, and one's identity and worldview are confronted, you can be sure the enemy will recant, using offense and pride, for example, to reinforce borders around a person or a region, in order to shield them from the entrance of *Light* or *Truth*.

Paul admonished those participating in such deception in Acts 14:15-16 (NKJV):

> Men, why are you doing these things? We also are men with the same nature as you and preach to you that you should turn from these useless things to the living God, who made the heaven, the earth, the sea, and all things that are in them, who in bygone generations allowed all nations to walk in their own ways.

In 2 Corinthians 6:17 (NKJV), we are instructed: "Come out from among them And be separate, says the Lord. Do not touch what is unclean, and I will receive you."

Jesus said of Himself that He is *the* Door in John 10:7-9 (NKJV), the legal entry point into the spiritual realm.

> Most assuredly, I say to you, I Am the Door of the sheep. All who ever came

before Me are thieves and robbers, but
the sheep did not hear them. I Am the
Door. If anyone enters by Me, he will be
saved, and will go in and out and find
pasture.

Jesus said very clearly in John 14:6 (NKJV): "I am the
Way, the Truth, and the Life. No one comes to the Father
except through Me."

He did not say that He was one way to God or "a" way.
But rather, The One and Only Way. Meaning all other ways
are leading to a wrong destination.

How Does Jesus Fit into the Life of a Native American?

On the other side of these non-negotiable truths is the
damage that has been done to Indigenous people groups at
the hands of those claiming to be followers of Christ. I have
already spoken in length, in Chapter 3, in this regard. *To
demand change in cultural practices that are not identified as
sin in the Bible as a condition of salvation is to proclaim a false
gospel.*

Therefore, the question still remains in the minds of
most Native American Christians to this day. Where do you
draw the line, so to speak? And, where do I fit in?

I want to recommend a book written by a pastor friend
of mine from South Dakota—Quincy Good Star. I believe
pastor Good Star provides the best explanations that I personally know of that answer the common questions regarding Native American tradition and Christianity. At least from
a Lakota people perspective.

If Jesus is God, what does this mean for Native American culture? This question is central to many Native American people. Good Star's book, titled *The Blue Road: Jesus Fulfills the Old Way*, differentiates culture from religion, thereby offering answers to this central question.

Good Star explains in detail that just as Jesus fulfilled the old Jewish covenant law given at Mount Sinai, He also fulfilled the traditional ways of the Lakota and Native American nations. He notes that many cultures, nations, and tribes are confused as to how to bridge the cultural gap of being a Native American and a Christian. He also addresses *the error of mixing native religion with Christianity* as well as the error of throwing out Native American culture, customs, and heritage altogether.

Good Star's book includes biblical insights as it pertains to Jesus fulfilling the Old Way with the New Covenant. He then applies these insights specifically to the sun dance, sweat lodge, making-of-relatives ceremony, naming ceremony, four directions, and smudging.

As for Me and My House

Just before Joshua died at the age of one hundred and ten years old, he assembled the Israelites and charged them with three choices, recorded in Joshua 24:14-15 (NIV). These same three choices are before each one of us today.

> Now fear the LORD and serve him with all faithfulness. Throw away the gods your ancestors worshiped beyond the Euphrates River and in Egypt and serve the LORD. But if serving the LORD

> seems undesirable to you, then choose for
> yourselves this day whom you will serve,
> whether the gods your ancestors served
> beyond the Euphrates, or the gods of the
> Amorites, in whose land you are living.
> But as for me and my household, we will
> serve the LORD.

The three choices are clear: Either serve the gods of your ancestors, or serve the gods in the land you are now living in (throughout America and the nations of the world, there are many), *or* serve the Lord.

It would be safe to say that all people have, in some way, shape, or form, strayed from Creator God in our religions, traditions, and man-made doctrines. Across the board, to some degree, whether in our churches, ministries, denominations, or customs, we, in large part, have turned away from the One True God.

Take lukewarmness, for example. God said He would vomit such out of His mouth (Revelation 3:16). Have we, in our religious piousness, sacrificed the fire of God in our hearts and churches for the doctrines of man? (Matthew 15:9) Do we give God lip service, yet our hearts are far from Him? (Matthew 15:8) Do we project a form of godliness but deny its power? (2 Timothy 3:5) Such sanctimonious, religious lifelessness is having a devastating effect on American Christianity and culture. This could be a subject for another whole book.

Cycles Perpetuate Until Someone Rises Up to Stop It

There is a story in 1 Kings 18:17-24 (NKJV) about a showdown between prophets and altars. The place was Mt. Carmel. The competitors were Yahweh's prophet Elijah and the false prophets of Baal.

> Ahab said to Elijah the prophet, "Is that you, O troubler of Israel? And Elijah answered saying, 'I have not troubled Israel, but you and your father's house have, in that you have forsaken [departed from, abandoned, renounced and neglected] the commandments [the ways] of the Lord and have followed after Balaam.'"
>
> Verses 17-18

The Message Translation states it this way: "You've dumped God's ways and commands and ran after the local gods" (Verse 18).

The effects of Solomon's syncretistic altar worship filtered down over time resulting in a severe drought in the land in Elijah's day. This drought affected every single area of Israel's life as it was an agricultural society, e.g., their ability to grow food or locate clean drinking water. *Elijah offered the spiritual reason for the physical problem*—God's chosen people were caught up in the culture of their day.

Their hearts were drawn away from the true God. They had become desensitized to the truth. In exchange, they substituted the worship of idols at satanic altars.

What are some possible implications for today from this Bible story? When a person, a family, a people, a nation, or a generation in any place forsakes or neglects God and His ways, *disaster is sure to follow.*

The idea that there is a direct link between the heart of man and the condition of the earth is a powerful one. Verse 21 continues, "And Elijah came to all the people, and said, 'How long will you falter between two opinions? If the Lord is God, follow Him; but if Baal, follow him.'" This story goes on in (1 Kings 18:30, NKJV) to say:

> Then Elijah repaired the altar of the Lord that was broken down. As a result of Godly altars being restored, the fire of the Lord fell and consumed the burnt sacrifice. When all the people saw it, they fell on their faces; and the said, The Lord—He is God!

When the altars were dealt with, there were results. A massive turning back of hearts to Yahweh and the execution of the false prophets of Baal.

Today, there are not literal prophets of Baal, but in the New Testament, the spirit of Baal is alive and well. However, God is never going to be outmatched by Baal. The power of God is always stronger than the power of darkness. The Spirit of Baal will always give rise to the spirit of Elijah, true prophets, and the people of God who will rebuild the broken-down altars of the Lord.

The Blood of Jesus at Calvary

I have experienced first-hand the effects of my heart being completely turned away from God. I have personally experienced how the power of darkness can hold one in bondage. But I also know the power of deliverance and freedom by and through an act of blood sacrifice at an altar. And that act has the potential to change *all* of humanity.

Let me assure you, there is absolute forgiveness in the precious atoning blood of Jesus Christ. This remains true whether you've had an abortion, or struggled with addiction, thereby losing your children to the foster care system. The same holds true whether you've been ensnared by a false religion, tradition, or man-made church doctrines. Christ's finished work on the cross at Calvary can totally eradicate the power and effects of the kingdom of darkness *and* restore what has been lost. As Hebrews 9:12 says, "Not with the blood of goats and calves, but with His own blood, He entered the Most Holy Place *once for all,* having *obtained eternal redemption."*

There was an altar at Calvary, and the *precious blood of Jesus* was poured out for your forgiveness and mine. He paid the ransom for the penalty of sin for you, this generation, and the nations. Jesus' blood far out-weighs any counterfeit altar worship that the enemy can ever erect. His blood will *never* lose its power, and it will *never* require more blood. It is *finished, and He is King!*

This powerful truth is for you and your children and your children's children. It's called "generational blessing." And friend, your enemy is shaking in his boots that you are reading this far. You can very well be the one in your family who rises up to break the cycle of bondage in your bloodline, in your generation, in your nation.

I believe we are the ones, and now is the time to arise in the spirit of Elijah for another showdown surrounding the high places of culture. Let us be secure in His finished work, declaring boldly; "You call on your gods, and we'll call upon the Name of the Lord, and the God who answers with fire, wins!"

It all begins with a true awakening. Allow me to tell you how the matters we have discussed in these few chapters were operating against my life and how a genuine encounter with this Man they call Jesus changed everything.

6

I Once Was Lost

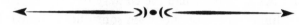

"If a man has a hundred sheep, and one of them goes astray,
does he not leave the ninety-nine and go to the mountains
to seek the one that is straying?"

~Matthew 18:12 (NKJV)~

I had a target on my back and didn't even know it. The power
of darkness searches for legal entry points, and my life was
wide open. My rebellion, pride, and wounded soul made for
easy access.

Methamphetamines came knocking, and when I
opened the door, he didn't come in alone. Wherever you see
meth, you will see other spirits attached to it, such as suicide,
murder, and the spirit of death. They all ride together like a
well-organized mob. Anger, rage, and domestic violence are
also a byproduct of this drug, and this was the case in my
own life.

My firstborn son, whom I had at just sixteen years old,
was not quite two when I was introduced to this demonic
drug. The devil himself came for me with a vengeance in this
dark period of my life. His agenda? To steal, kill and destroy.

Because of this drug and alcohol abuse, I can recall one
specific occasion of physical assault and domestic violence. It
happened while my two-year-old son was asleep in the living
room. There was a crowd of male friends, just in the next

room, who did nothing. Why? Because it was considered normal. Satan has used this particularly evil drug to devastate so many families today, and I can relate.

Domestic violence against women is considered common among certain people groups. That night as the partying continued, I finally had the courage to call 911. I was so scared I hung up the phone when someone answered. Even so, the police eventually showed up at the front door. They took one look at me, and they put him in jail for physical assault.

However, he was only in jail long enough for the door to be open to another sad situation. I ended up pregnant for the second time. When you are living in darkness, you are vulnerable at every turn. When you choose to live your life outside the confines and protection of God, or even just ignorant to the truth of the Gospel, you are living in a perpetual danger zone. Sadly, my story is all too familiar and "not-as-bad" as so many who are sitting in the darkness of their captivity.

The enemy took what already hurt in my life as a child and used that pain as an opening to have his way with me. His assignment was to systematically tear me down until I had not one drop of self-worth left. He was to make sure I was convinced I was worthless.

My sin, rebellion, and ignorance made me easy prey. He wanted to chisel away at me until he reached my center core so that I would identify as hopeless and orphaned. Ungodly strongholds were mounting around me and being reinforced quickly. To the core of my belief system, I agreed that I was "nothing special," "nothing good could ever happen," and "this is just how it is for me." I truly believed that *not even God could want me.*

This is what is going on today for the mothers and fathers of the children at NAOMI House and foster homes around the world. Families, communities, and young people are fighting this demonic drug and other addictions that have enormous strength. The kingdom of darkness is infiltrating our cities, streets, and reservations, literally carrying out marching orders like that of a highly organized gang, destroying any life or family in its path. Perpetuating the sins of their mothers and fathers to the next generation, it is the children who are especially vulnerable and unprotected.

Even in the midst of my own personal hell, I knew I didn't want to partake in hard drugs while pregnant. It was the saving grace of this pregnancy that allowed me to step away from meth, for good, miraculously. This is how my mother's prayers were working. I didn't plan on becoming pregnant, but it saved my life.

I knew that I would never be able to care for another child, so I called my caseworker, who counseled me with my first son. I hadn't talked to her in a long time. I knew she was a very loving, Christian, concerned woman. I dialed the number, and she answered, "Hello?" Quietly I said, "Hi, this is Genevieve." She said, "Hi, Genevieve!" with cheer in her voice. I was quiet. She spoke again, with deep compassion, "Genevieve, are you okay? Are you pregnant?" I said, "Yes," and began to cry.

I carried my precious son for nine months, and on the day of delivery, I knew that I would be giving him up for adoption. I couldn't bear the idea of bringing a new baby into the mess of a life that I had made.

After his birth, he had to be in the hospital for several days for jaundice. I went to visit him every day and fed him and kissed him all over his beautiful face. I'll never forget his smell. Truly heavenly. Looking back, I believe the nurses may have been angels. They were so kind to me. I know they had to have felt sorry for me.

Because of some ICWA laws and tribal issues involved in my case concerning adoption, my son had to go into a Foster Home for thirty days until a court hearing was held. After the courts released him, it was time to meet with that nice social worker, my mother, and my three-year-old son at the adoption agency. The adoptive mom and dad met us there too.

When the foster mom brought in my baby that day, I burst into tears. I kissed him and smelled him and held him. He had gotten so chunky in just one month!

I was so young. Just nineteen. I was far from being a Christian, but I knew everyone else in the room was, and I respected that. As they started to pray, my mind traveled back into the basement of the little Assembly of God church that we had grown up in. I remembered hearing about Jesus that He loved me. I remembered completely rejecting Him, too, going my own way and doing my own thing. Look where I ended up. He, God, definitely wouldn't want me now, was my conclusion.

They finished their prayers as I held my precious little boy and realized it was time to go. Everyone was frozen. They didn't know what to say or do. So, I just stood up and walked over to the new mother, who, to this day, I remember the look of awe, and probably some fear, on her face. I handed my bundle of love into her arms, I kissed him on the forehead, and I walked out of that building without him, tears streaming down my face. (see Photo #7 on page 242)

When I was in the parking lot, I saw their vehicle. Minnesota license plates. The car was filled to the brim with so much "baby stuff!" All the things I knew I could never provide, and I said to myself, "you made the right choice."

I went back to my lifestyle and continued to spiral down the road of heavy alcoholism, hopelessness, grief, and a deep sense of emptiness.

This is what led me to make the most desperate and sad decision yet, less than a year later.

"Dad, I need money for an abortion." It wasn't until I really sat down to think about these events that my mind wandered all the way back to my father pulling me to the side when I discovered I was pregnant with my first son, Joshua. "You've chosen a hard path, Genevieve. It is going to be very difficult to have a child so young, and I want you to know that you have options." I wasn't sure what he was talking about. At sixteen years old, taking the life of my unborn child was something that had simply never crossed my mind. Nor was it anything I was willing to consider.

Unfortunately, just four short years later, my father's offer still stood. He wired me the money by the afternoon. I was only twenty years old when I arrived at the clinic to terminate this pregnancy.

I became more steeped in self-hatred, emptiness, and worthlessness than ever before. Alcohol was the only way I could block out my decision and what happened in that clinic. If I hadn't yet stepped over into the abyss of "no-return" back to God, I now knew I had crossed it. Or so I believed these things to be true, way deep down in my soul.

I'm Moving to Phoenix

That spring, after taking a road trip to Phoenix with some girlfriends—for all the wrong reasons—I decided to flee South Dakota and move to Arizona as a young single mother. Surely life would be better if I change geographical locations!

There was a phrase my mother used to tell me that resounded in my head like nails on the chalkboard of my rebellious mind. She would say, "Honey, no matter where you go, there you are." Oh, that used to drive me crazy, yet how very true it is. I didn't realize that it wasn't external circumstances that were causing me such anguish. It was the trauma of my soul and my desperate need to be connected to the life-giving power of Creator. The very Source of all life. I didn't know that if I was reconnected and restored on the inside, everything on the outside of my life would begin to change.

"I'm moving to Phoenix," I announced to my friends matter-of-factly. And I did. I packed up my little hatchback car with me and my four-year-old's belongings in garbage bags and drove the fifteen hours to 27th Avenue and Indian School.

Life in Phoenix proved to be just as rough and even harder in many ways! I was all alone. No family. No friends. No help. It was during this time that my mother was attending Oglala Lakota College on the reservation in South Dakota. My father was in a rehab center for drugs and alcohol there in Phoenix, and I would learn that just two short years later, he would go to bed and never wake up. It was also at this time that I learned of the tragic death of his brother, my uncle, who jumped off of a building in South Carolina.

I was holding down any temp job I could find, yet barely surviving. I was heavily addicted to alcohol and snorting enough cocaine to keep the entire neighborhood high. Anything that would help alleviate the pain and anguish in my soul. I soon found myself in another unhealthy relationship. When he started punching the walls, I knew I was next.

It was then that I remember crying out to my mothers' God in prayer for perhaps the first time in my life. I remember I spoke "in prayer" to a God who I wasn't sure existed, "God, if you are real. I need an apartment of my own."

Within a month of that prayer, I had my own little studio apartment. I remember connecting that apartment to my prayer. People came out of the woodwork to help me. I know they probably felt sorry for me. I quickly realized, though, I could not afford to live as a single mother in this huge city on my own. I asked my baby sister to move to Phoenix. At nineteen years old, she drove her little five-speed Hyundai Accent all the way from Maryland to Phoenix to live with me and "help."

We ended up not being too good for each other. Both of us were so wounded, hemorrhaging with the pain of father-lessness and the loss of identity. We were both addicts and couldn't get enough of everything that was dark.

My sister was working as a waitress one afternoon when she met someone who just so happened to attend a church very close to where we lived. Yes, a church. She called me from work, "Genevieve, I met this guy, and he invited me to his church on Sunday." I was groggy from drinking the night before when I asked, "What does he do?" We need food and rent, you know. She replied, "He's a youth pastor."

I just remember thinking, that's weird. I figured if my little sister moved all the way to Phoenix to help me not be on the street, the least I could do is go to church with her. And it is the only reason why we rolled up into the parking lot that Sunday morning.

Don't ever stop praying for your children. Just as my wrong choices and bitter attitudes left me vulnerable to darkness, likewise, the power of prayer and an interceding mother was putting a different kind of target on my back. There is power in prayer. My mother's sleepless nights of prayer and crying out to God for her children had located me in Phoenix and was getting ready to arrest me in my tracks.

7

Encounter Versus Religion

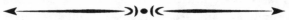

"Whether He is a sinner or not I do not know.
All I know is that once I was blind, and now, I can see,
For the first time in my life!"

~John 9:25 (TPT)~

Friends, only a true encounter with the living God has the power to open the eyes of our understanding of who He is. I can't tell you how many times I heard about Jesus, and it went in one ear and right out the other. Mostly what I remember hearing was that if you sin, you are going to hell. I knew I was a sinner. I didn't need the preacher to tell me that.

It wasn't *what* I didn't know. It was *Whom* I didn't know. And I was about to encounter Him. The Merriam-Webster Dictionary defines "encounter" as: "To experience, especially unexpectedly, to come upon face-to-face." Without experiential knowledge or divine revelation, man is merely groping in the darkness of our theological perceptions, religious opinions, and possible misconceptions of who He really is.

Lifeless, powerless religion or man-made tradition cannot connect you to Creator. Religion is a form of Antichrist. It is an anti-anointing spirit that yokes its prey with laborious efforts of measuring up—all to no avail. This yoke is closely followed up with spirits of guilt, shame, and big doses of condemnation for good measure—a continual sense of disconnectedness. Yuck. Who wants to just go through the motions?

In all of our intercession, in all of our crying out, our prayer must be that this generation truly *encounters* a revelation of Him, who restores honor and purity, making us part of His family. We must pray according to Ephesians 1:18: "The eyes of your understanding being enlightened; that you may know what is the hope of His calling is, what are the riches of the glory of His inheritance in the saints."

For me, that *encounter* happened in the parking lot of a little church in the middle of Phoenix, Arizona.

I remember it like it was yesterday. My life to that point had been a perpetual train wreck. I was coming in from off the street—completely broken, utterly helpless. Hopeless, really.

A Collision with Truth

Someone met me there that day, right there in that parking lot. Someone that you couldn't see, nor could you deny. It was God Himself—His anointing; His Spirit; His breathe; His *love!* This Presence was more powerful than all of my deep-rooted hatred. This love was more potent than all of my sin, and I was absolutely overcome.

His Presence was enveloping me in what I now know was an atmosphere of His Glory. I had fallen so far from His glory (all have sinned and fallen short of the glory) and was cut-off and estranged to His love. Without Him, I was just like the walking dead. Oh, I was alive on the outside but barren, lifeless, desolate, and empty on the inside.

As soon as we stepped out of our car that transformational morning, the volunteers were shaking our hands, smiling, and being so friendly. I wondered what's going on here? What kind of place is this? What do they want from me?"

As we were ushered closer and closer to the front doors, you could hear the most amazing gospel choir—the sound of praise, of worship, the sound of life. The frequency of that sound permeated every fiber of my soul, and I was almost trembling under the power of God's intoxicating presence.

I don't know if you know how it feels to be in church for the first time in a *long* time. I could literally feel my demons screaming! Those spirits who had taken up residency in my heart, life, and body knew what was coming with every step I took. They knew they would not be able to withstand wave after wave of God's glory.

I remember hearing voices telling me to *run.* "Get out of here. You don't belong here. You don't belong in the presence of God. You're dirty, remember? These aren't your kind of people. You are worthless. These people are holy and clean."

Honestly, those greeters shaking my hand all the way to being seated is one of the reasons I didn't run out of the church that morning into the familiar embrace and false security of my self-medicated pain, addiction, and hopelessness. They kept shaking my hand, smiling, and leading me forward. With each "Good morning" and "Hello," I could feel tears running down my face. All of my defenses were being systematically dismantled, and I was weeping under the power and conviction of the Holy Ghost. I could barely contain myself.

We were pushed in and seated closely together, right in the front. As I looked down our row to the left and to the right, I noticed we were surrounded by a row of mommas praying in the Holy Ghost, and I knew it was going down *today!* Today is the day of salvation (2 Corinthians 6:2), *not* tomorrow! Not next week! Today! The light and life of heaven collided with the darkness of my soul and the deadness of my spirit that day. The many years of my mother's prayers and intercessions had caught up with me.

A young preacher got up to speak with such an anointing (I didn't know what it was at the time), and I tell you what, it was a lot like Paul on the Road to Damascus. Acts 9 talks about the Apostle Paul (Saul) as he journeyed on the road near Damascus. A light was shown around him from heaven. He fell to the ground and heard a voice saying to him, "Why do you persecute me?" Paul's response? "Who are You, Lord?" Jesus made Himself known. He revealed Himself to Paul, and Paul was never, ever the same again. Trembling and astonished, Paul said, "Lord, what do You want me to do?"

One encounter can change everything. At the end of the sermon, they asked if anyone wanted to ask Jesus into their heart. I couldn't get out of the row fast enough. "Excuse me!" "Excuse me!" If that's Him, if that's the real Jesus, I need Him. If He wants me, I'm His. If He's real, give Him to me!

My sister and I rushed down the aisle that day. I repeated the sinner's prayer, and the preacher assured me I would never be the same again. I don't think he, or I, knew just how true that would be.

They led us to a room where they asked us if we wanted to be filled with the Holy Spirit and pray in tongues. I said to myself, "You don't know where I live. I need absolutely everything that I can get." They read some Scriptures about it, including a passage from Luke where it says if a man being evil knows how to give good gifts, how much more will your heavenly Father give the Holy Spirit to those who ask (11:13). I said to myself, "If He can save me from my sin, then surely He could do anything." I believed Him.

They led me in a simple prayer and instructed me to open not only my heart but my mouth, my voice box, and allow God to fill my breathe and begin to speak through me.

I was gloriously baptized in the Holy Spirit and prayed in other tongues, and I have never stopped in all of these years. It was a way to open up the reservoir of God's Spirit given to me upon salvation and release rivers of living water outward. As Acts 1:8 says, "You shall receive *power,* after that the Holy Ghost has come upon you to be a witness."

Looking back on all of the amazing things that happened to me that day, one thing I am so grateful for is that they were bold enough to ask me to be filled with the Holy Spirit. I had no problem doing that because no one told me I couldn't.

It wasn't until years after this incredible *encounter* that religion tried to tell me something different. But you cannot deny someone's testimony. It is not theology that will change anyone. Rather, it is an encounter and experiential knowledge of God's written Word that has the power to transform.

The truth is, when Jesus walked this earth, the religious systems of the day were openly challenged and condemned by Him. Jesus did not come to reform or renew the Old Way. He came to overturn the demonically energized religious systems of His day and completely replace them with Himself. He came to establish a completely new way of relating with God. First Corinthians 11:25 (NKJV) states, "This cup is the New Covenant in My Blood."

A Man Born Blind

I love the story in John chapter 9 that talks about a man born blind. Jesus rubbed dirt and saliva together, placed His hands on his eyes, and the man received a miracle of sight.

Everyone questioned the man. He was brought before the Pharisees for interrogation since this miraculous sign of healing was performed on a sabbath day which was against religious law. If he professed Jesus as the Christ, he could be cast out of the synagogue for good. The healed man told them what had happened through the hands of a *man named Jesus*.

The religious rulers were perplexed and disgusted! "How were your eyes opened? Who was he? How did he do this? We know this man is a sinner!" The formerly blind man's response in the face of the hardened bunch of pious hypocrites is found in verse 25, and it gives me chills every time I read it. The Passion translation records his response: "I have no idea what kind of man he is. All I know is that once I was blind, and now, I can see for the first time in my life!"

This is the power of encounter, and the blind man defines the condition of humanity without it. We were all born blind. We were all born in sin and iniquity. As the Psalmist says, "Behold, I was brought forth in iniquity, and in sin my mother conceived me" (51:5).

I had lived my entire life to that point "all in" for the power of darkness. I met a Man named Jesus who touched my eyes and healed my understanding of who He is. From that day forth, I would be "all in" for the kingdom of God.

> *Grace, Grace, Amazing Grace*
> "Once I was lost. But now I'm found.
> I was blind, but now I see."
>
> "You who once were far off, have been brought
> near by the precious blood of Jesus."
>
> ~Ephesians 2:1 (NKJV)~

Again, the *only* power the enemy has is to slander or deceive. Deception means no light or the ability to keep something hidden or covered over. The antidote to deception is a revelation, which means to take the cover off; let the light shine into the darkness.

That day when I encountered the power of God, there were a couple of revelations that burst open for me to understand. And I believe one *encounter* can help anyone receive these truths.

Absolute Forgiveness

I recall hearing many, many Scriptures about the forgiveness of sin growing up in my mom's little church, such as:

> "As far as the east is from the west, so far hath He removed our transgressions (guilt) from us" (Psalm 103:12, NKJV).

> "I, even I, Am He who blots out your transgressions for My own sake; and I will not remember your sins" (Isaiah 43:25, NKJV).

> "Though your sins are like scarlet, they shall be as white as snow" (Isaiah 1:18, NKJV).

But on *this* day? On this day, the Word of God came to life, and the lights were turned on for me. My eyes were *opened.*

Hebrews 4:12 says that "The Word of God is alive, powerful and sharper than any two-edged sword." The Message translation says that His Word is "sharper than a surgeon's scalpel."

This means the living Word has the power to do serious surgery. The living Word of God will cut out the poison of sin from your life and rearrange everything that is in chaos so as to make us a place for His presence to dwell or take up residency. It was at this moment that I knew God had forgiven me of everything. My rebellion, hard-heartedness, self-hatred, addiction. Everything. I knew with everything within me that His blood had washed me clean.

A true encounter with God has the ability to translate us from religious Sunday morning rituals or traditional ceremonies that attempt to "make us worthy" to life-giving transformation—cleansing us and making us a holy vessel from the inside out.

There is a difference between hearing with your natural ears and the opening of the eyes of your understanding. When the Holy Spirit takes the cover off and unveils the Truth contained in Scripture, you are set free. "You shall *know* the truth, and the truth shall make you free" (John 8:32). The word "know" here means intimate or experiential knowledge. When this happens, no devil in hell can ever bring it back up to you again in order to bring guilt, shame, or self-condemnation because it is *lost* forever in the sea of eternal forgetfulness!

Righteousness in Him Alone

This encounter with the Lord will help us to realize we do not (we cannot) clean *ourselves* up. Christianity is the only religion that doesn't require that you come to God. He came to and for *us!*

This revelation was so life-changing and vivid. I remember that very morning that I received Christ. I could almost physically see a white robe of righteousness descend down upon my life. I knew that I was completely and entirely made righteous. I was clean, made pure before my Creator, and boldness came upon my life. I knew that I was standing completely cleansed in the blood of Christ. Hebrews 4:16 was crazy amazing, saying we (me, *you*) can "come boldly to the throne of grace to obtain mercy and find help in a time of need." *Wow!* Meaning we can walk right up to God and talk to Him! The same is true for *every* believer.

Whether you feel clean or not, that does *not* change the truth. We can approach God because we are accepted by Him; His Son tightly embraces us; His favor has been restored to us. And He did not accomplish this by taking us on a guilt trip. No! Romans 2:4 (NKJV) reminds us, "It is the goodness of God that leads you unto repentance" (that is, to change your inner self, your old way of thinking—seek His purpose for your life). When we taste and see for ourselves that He is oh, so good (Psalm 34:8), it causes any bad taste in our mouth towards Him caused by religion or ignorance to be removed.

Baptism of the Holy Spirit

Immediately after receiving this gift of Christ in my life, I was subsequently filled with the baptism of the Holy Spirit with the biblical evidence of praying in another language. "If you then, being evil, know how to give good gifts to your children, how much more will your heavenly Father give the Holy Spirit to those who ask Him!" (Luke 11:13, NKJV)

It was so crystal clear. I knew I was evil. And I knew I loved my children. I knew my heavenly Father was perfect and that He would give me, His daughter, what I needed. I just believed it.

That same day I asked God to fill me with His Holy Spirit's fullness to empower me to live for Him and fulfill His purpose forever. I took a deep breath and began to speak in another language as the Spirit gave me utterance (Acts 2:1). I know that is where the fiery boldness comes from that rests upon my life today (Acts 1:8).

Paul's Damascus encounter launched him into the ministry *after* being *filled with the Holy Spirit.*

> And Ananias entered the house; and laying hands on him he said "Brother Saul, the Lord Jesus, who appeared to you on the road as you came, has sent me that you may receive your sight and be filled with the Holy Spirit." Immediately there fell from his eyes something like scales, and he received his sight at once; and he arose and was baptized.
>
> Acts 9:17-18 (NKJV)

Paul then went to the synagogues he was on his way to persecute but instead proclaimed Jesus (Acts 9:20).

Perfectly Loved and Created on Purpose for a Purpose

"Perfect love casts off all fear!" (1 John 4:18, NKJV) I could hardly believe that not only was I not a throwaway but that God had a plan, a purpose, and a pre-determined destiny for my life. "Before I formed you in the womb, I knew you. Before you were born, I sanctified you; I ordained you a prophet to the nations" (Jeremiah 1:5, NKJV). I wasn't totally sure what He had pre-ordained for me to do, but I was absolutely convinced that He had. I was determined to find out what it was and pursue it wholeheartedly. Jeremiah 29:11 was a deeply engrained reality for me: "I know the plan that I think toward you saith the Lord, plans of good and not of evil, to give you a future and a hope."

When you *know* you are forgiven, you *know* you are clothed in white robes of righteousness before the Creator of the Universe. You *know* that you are perfectly accepted and loved, and you didn't do anything to deserve it or earn it! When the Holy Spirit comes upon your life and lights you up, honey, a *new* kind of boldness comes upon your life. It's a new creature in Christ kind of boldness that lets hell know you should've stopped me when you had a chance. But now? Oh, now it's game on. I'm giving my life over to King Jesus for now and for good, and we're coming back for a generation!

That's the day my life shifted from a *mess* to a *message,* from a daughter of darkness to a child of the Light; from *outcast* to *adopted,* from *lost* to *found.* Once I was blind, and like Saul, who became Paul, now I can see.

Concluding Reflections

Religion strives to serve deity out of guilt, rooted in fear, in an attempt to measure up and appease or "get to" God.

True salvation could be described as the ability, or grace, to comprehend, through divine revelation (encounter), that Jesus paid the price for my unworthiness. The understanding and acceptance of this kind of love, this level of mercy, transforms the hardest of hearts.

This invitation to relationship, full partnership with the Creator of all things, empowers us to walk in complete devotion to Him.

How About You?

How about you? The reason I can so confidently ask you this question is that, as I described, Jesus revealed Himself to me. Truly there is no way that you can meet Him and then not offer Him to everyone around you.

I want to encourage you to talk to Him, right there, wherever you are reading. Let Him know that you want to know Him too. Ask Him to reveal Himself to you in a personal way. Ask Him to come alive on the inside of you and help you follow Him all the days of your life.

Ask Him for a fresh revelation or encounter of His love and His presence today.

Pray with me:

"Father God, I come before You in the Name of Your Son, Jesus Christ.

Today, I invite You, Jesus, into my heart and life as Lord and Savior. I know that I am a sinner, and I ask You for forgiveness. I believe that You are the way, the truth, and the life. I believe You died for my sins and rose from the dead.

God, I ask You to fill me with Your Holy Spirit and empower me to live for you and walk with You all the days of my life. I ask You, Father, for a fresh revelation of Your love for me.

In Jesus' name, I pray. Amen."

8

I Will Go Where You Want Me to Go

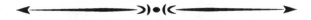

"You are the God who does wonders;
You have declared Your strength among the peoples."

~Psalm 77:14 (NKJV) ~

After my powerful encounter and conversion, I was totally set free from drugs and alcohol overnight. God was working in me so powerfully by the preaching and teaching of His word.

I enrolled in the Layperson's Bible School that my church offered, and I literally soaked up every word being taught by some very anointed ministers and teachers. I had an insatiable appetite for God's living word. His word began to jump off the pages and stitch my life back together again, piece by piece.

Obviously, we should never stop growing no matter how long we have been Christian, but it is so vital as a new believer. First Peter 2:2 in the New Living Translations says: "Like newborn babies, you must crave pure spiritual milk so that you will grow into a full experience of salvation. Cry out for this nourishment."

This is not a burdensome truth. We have the privilege of delving into the scriptures, with the Holy Spirit as our personal guide who turns on the lights and reveals Christ to us in all 66 books.

I was taught that I needed to "plug in" to some type of volunteer service. I became an usher, shaking people's hands, welcoming them into the service. "Good morning!" "Praise the Lord!" "Thank You, Jesus!" "Halleluiah!" I served God with all my heart, soul, and strength, *right where I was planted.*

The people of God I was connected to showed me how to "get a hold of God" for myself. I remember my Pastor explaining it like this. You can catch a fish, clean it, prepare it, and serve it and that man will eat real good for a day. But if you teach that man (or woman) how to fish, he will never go hungry again.

I was being prepared for the ministry.

He Shall Live and Not Die!

As I mentioned, my church knew how to train up disciples and equip the saints. After living a lifetime unto the worship of "self," I was now living to serve others and sit down under the teaching and ministry of the Word. I was quickly learning how to pray and intercede, how to share my faith, and lead people to salvation. I was growing in the Lord and in faith in His Word and promises.

As brand-new Christians, my roommate and I were entrusted as "small group" leaders out of our little apartment in Phoenix. We started praying and interceding for our whole apartment complex and saw people get saved and healed.

One night, there was a shooting in the apartment above us. A group of people had been partying all night long when a fight broke out, and shots were fired. A bullet hit Christopher, our neighbor upstairs. At about 3:00 a.m., there was pounding at our front door. An FBI agent wanted to question us. Blood from Christopher's body had poured down into our front porch. They said he had been transported to the hospital, but that was all they told us.

We were three roommates full of the Holy Ghost and on fire for God. Acts 1:8 (KJV) says, "But ye shall receive power, after that the Holy Ghost is come upon you." We did what came naturally. After the police officers left, we walked around our apartment praying in the Holy Ghost, crying out to God in intercession for Christopher's life and soul. We prayed this way for several hours until it was time to take our kids to school in the morning. We walked out and managed to get around all the yellow tape strewed around our apartment to get our kids to class.

We then went directly to the community hospital. I bet you we were beaming with the light of God's Glory after all the praying we had done all night. We found our way into the hospital, and miraculously we were allowed to go right to the waiting room outside where the emergency surgery was taking place. Once we got into the waiting room, we saw a room full of people who we knew were Christopher's family members. We were lit up! We were directed to an older lady, his grandmother, who had raised Christopher since he was a little boy. She was weeping and clinging to the rosary in her hand with desperation in her eyes.

We walked right up to her and told her in a very excitable and energized frenzy, "We have been praying all night! God says your grandson is going to live and not die! He is going to declare the wonderful works of the Lord!" She was pretty hysterical, to say the least. She managed to say through her frantic tears of shock, "Oh my God! You all must be angels," We hugged and prayed for her. We boldly declared, "He will live!" And then we left.

I tell you what. That young man made a miraculous recovery from a gunshot wound to the head. There was so much swelling in his brain he should not have survived. If he had survived, he should have been a vegetable. What a mighty God!

He wasn't in the hospital very long, and when he got home, his grandmother invited us to come to see her grandson. Of course, he had heard about us. He greeted us at the door and gave us a hug. His speech was very slurred, and he had lost some mobility but was expected to regain all his faculties over time, and he did. We learned that he had struggled as a drug addict for years, as well as had spent most of his juvenile and young adult years incarcerated.

We ministered to him about Jesus, and within a week, that young man was taking that same journey down to the altar to receive Jesus as His savior at my little church, just like I had, not very long before. He gave his life to the Lord that day.

I truly believe that testimonies like this should be the *norm* and not the exception. We were simply carrying out our "marching orders" that were clearly laid out for us by our superiors. We were trained and deployed into our neighborhood, representing our Chief commanding officer, Jesus Christ. We were brand new Christian converts. We didn't know any different, and I am so glad we didn't.

This is how it was in the book of Acts, *and* it is how it should be for the Christian church today.

Equipping the Saints for the Work of the Ministry

Ephesians 4:11-12(NKJV) describes the duty of the five-fold ministry of the apostles, prophets, evangelists, pastors, and teachers: *"for the equipping of the saints for the work of ministry, for the edifying of the body of Christ."*

There is a natural progression that should take place when we are brought into the family of the kingdom of God. The Bible says: "Those who are planted in the house of the Lord Shall flourish in the courts of our God" (Psalm 92:13, NKJV). Flourish here means to burst forth, bud or sprout, to blossom and grow.

However, the reverse of this truth as well. That is, if we are rootless, we will remain fruitless. Mark 4:17 talks about it, saying: "And they have no root in themselves, and so endure only for a time. Afterward, when tribulation or persecution arises for the word's sake, immediately they stumble." God never promised walking the Christian walk would be easy. He promised He would never leave us to walk it alone.

I encourage you here. Get planted in a Bible teaching, Holy Spirit-led church, and don't allow anything to uproot you prematurely. Obviously, seasons change, and there are surely times the Holy Spirit will move you from one place to another. However, know the difference! We cannot afford to allow negative past experiences, "church hurt," or offense to keep us from being planted and experiencing the fruit of growth. Discern if the Holy Spirit led you to a certain place and then remain!

I can pretty much guarantee that even with the powerful conversion I had, if afterward, I were to be disconnected from the Body of Christ or left to my own devices, I would have never made it out of my past alive. My testimony very well could have been 2 Peter 2:22, "A dog returns to his own vomit, and a wow, having washed, to her wallowing in the mire."

Discipleship is a two-way road. We must have those who will teach, train, and equip us (Ephesians 4:11), but we must remain humble, hungry, teachable, accountable, and planted.

I know I could never repay Jesus for the debt He paid, but I can tell you Psalm 84:10 (NKJV) describes my heart of gratitude, declaring:

> For a day in Your courts is better than a thousand [anywhere else]; I would rather be a doorkeeper and stand at the threshold in the house of my God Than dwell [at ease] in the tents of wickedness.

The Message Version says: "I'd rather scrub floors in the house of my God than be honored as a guest in the palace of sin."

Listen. I have scrubbed many floors. Washed many toilets. Changed many diapers. All in serving the Lord. But realize this; when your motivation to serve is Colossians 3:23 (NKJV): "And whatever you do, do it heartily (with all of your heart), as to the Lord and not to men"—know this; you are being positioned, groomed, and developed for leadership in God's kingdom affairs.

Soldiers in God's Army

In the kingdom, the path that leads to the top is only found when your life is laid down prostrate before the Lord and then stay there. You really cannot bring *all* of you with, where God is taking you. The higher we desire to rise in the things of the spirit, the lower we must live in the things of the flesh. When we live unto the Lord like this, we are entrusted with His glorious power and ability to flow with the miraculous.

There are many similarities between Christian growth and military rank. When God's word commands us to be humble, or submit, or serve, or prefer others above self, or walk in the fruit of the spirit, be accountable, etc., it is not because these are powerless, degrading, or pointless disciplines. It is because as a soldier in the army of the Lord, there is a literal chain of command in the spirit.

This is not difficult to understand in the military. There are requirements, basic training, and boot camp. The military is full of strict orders and structure, which all provide *protection* and *delegated authority* to the soldier. So it is, in the kingdom, and our enemy knows our rank.

The Lord gave me an example of the importance of Godly order and spiritual covering. He showed me a Ferris Wheel, as you see at the county fair. You get onto the ride, and then you move slowly upward, to the top, and then back down to the lowest level. This is a picture of the cycle of *submission to* and *walking in* authority. "Humble yourselves under the mighty hand of God that He may exalt you in due time" (1 Peter 5:6, NKJV). In other words, you cannot walk in authority without being humbly submitted under authority.

Many people want to experience greater levels of spiritual authority, faith and answered prayer, but they have yet to get on the ride. When Jesus entered the village of Capernaum, a captain in the Roman army approached him, requesting a miracle.

> Lord, he said, "I have a son who is lying in my home, paralyzed and suffering terribly." Jesus responded, "I will go with you and heal him." But the Roman officer interjected, "Lord, who am I to have you come into my house? *I understand your authority*, for I too am a man who *walks under authority* and *have authority over* soldiers who serve under me. I can tell one to go and he'll go, and another to come and he'll come. I order my servants and they'll do whatever I ask. *So, I know that all you need to do is stand here and command healing* over my son and he will be instantly healed." Jesus was astonished when He heard this and said to those who were following Him, "He has greater faith than anyone I've encountered in Israel!"

Matthew 8:6-10 (The Passion Version)

There is something to be said about the Centurion soldier's ability to recognize and operate in a chain of command. Because he understood this principle, he could easily recognize Jesus' *spiritual rank*. This understanding afforded him access to the realm of the miraculous, and it made Jesus marvel.

The Leadership Test

Ultimately, it matters very little who it is that God has called you to submit to, whether they are qualified or competent or the best choice. What matters is this—will you pass *the Leadership Test?*

Accepting and living out this wisdom truth is a process, and we will have plenty of opportunities for practice as there are many authorities. Every believer must learn this principle of Godly submission to all authorities over our lives if we wish to advance. Promotion does not always come in title or accolades, but it is a definite elevation in rank in the spirit realm.

Submission is for our protection. Without it, we can easily open the door to enemy encroachment as we are operating illegally. I am surely not talking about submitting to sin or ridiculous and willful acts against God and His Word.

Certainly, there are those in leadership who unfortunately abuse their power and the people they are called to lead. Please do not hear what I am not saying. I am not talking about submitting and connecting to abusive, sinful people or situations. Sheesh. There is a line between authentic connection and the "bizarre," and surely both are out there. What I am saying is—being connected, rooted, and grounded in the Body of Christ, in fellowship with believers, is God's blueprint for our continual growth and developing fruit in the things of God. One way to say it is—don't be a "lone-ranger."

Realize extreme independence, discord, and self-governance can stop the flow of God's power upon our lives. Walls of self-protection may need to come down, as they can block and hinder the flow. Our ability to receive and execute orders in the natural correlates with the spiritual.

Maybe you have experienced abuse by an authority in some way, shape, or form. Maybe you have your own deep wounds of rejection and abandonment that re-surface each time you try to connect yourself with others in the Body of Christ. Recognize it is the enemy behind this, whose goal is to get us to throw the genuine benefit of Godly structure out the window. However, the results of living disconnected, unsubmitted and individualistically, can be dangerous. Sadly, there have been many needless casualties of war in the kingdom through isolation. There is safety in numbers.

Make sure it is the Holy Spirit that has planted you where you are, and then trust the process. There will be many emotional ups and downs, highs and lows, but the decision to operate in "the fear of the Lord," and not your own power, will be your firm grip during the ride.

The Fear of the Lord

To walk in the fear of the Lord speaks of doing all that you do as unto God and not unto man (Colossians 3:23) while honoring and submitting to those in authority over you.

We don't talk about Godly fear much, but it is the beginning of wisdom (Proverbs 9:10). Here's a definition of the fear of the Lord to reflect on—to actively reverence and respect God in the way that we conduct our lives. A surrendered life of radical obedience and service to God is powerful.

Here is what the Lord spoke to me in prayer one day. He said, *"The enemy is only required to fear you to the degree that you walk in the fear of the Lord."* Read that again.

The prospect of you becoming discipled and authentically developed to bear fruit in God's kingdom is the devil's worst nightmare. Where there are a people of God gathered and unified, God commands the blessing there, and the anointing will flow from the top down (Psalm 133:1-2).

Honestly? There are no skipping steps when it comes to things of the kingdom. The kingdom is a counterculture. When you are weak, you are endued with His strength. To go up, you must remain low (humble). Give first, and then it will be given, etc. Learning to obey God in the small things, as Matthew 25:21 (NKJV) admonishes, results in an increase: *"You were faithful over a few things, I will make you ruler over many things."*

I will speak of this more in a later chapter, but for now, I must share this testimony of the miracle-working power of God that healed my body.

You Are Who You Say You Are

One day, very shortly after my salvation experience, I was sitting at the breakfast table with my son when suddenly, out of nowhere, I was struck with such severe pain in my lower back, I dropped to the floor. I was in so much pain. I could hardly move. How was I going to get to work? How would I get my son to school? I literally could not walk.

I went to see a chiropractor who basically said I was born with a sciatica nerve issue that would never go away for the rest of my life, but with enough treatments, I could learn to live with it and not have so much pain. This was devastating news. I was way too young to have lower back issues, and I needed to get to work!

The following day the pain was even worse. I had to scoot on my bottom down the apartment flight of stairs, and somehow, I was able to drive down to my little church. I begged the pastor to pray for me because I needed to get to work that afternoon! They told me Jesus heals, and I needed a miracle. To my utter disappointment, the pastor prayed a quick prayer and then handed me a tape. This tape was a recording of Kenneth E. Hagin reciting every Scripture on healing out loud from the Bible from Genesis to Revelation.

I wondered, what am I going to do with this? You see, I was working a temp job. If I don't go to work, I don't get paid. If I don't get paid, my son and I are liable to be on the street. I was mad. I grabbed the tape and left for the painful ride home, scooting back up my stairs and laying on my apartment floor. I just wept. I was in pain. I was scared. Where is Jesus now? Reluctantly I put that tape in and pushed play. Sure enough, there was this voice repeating verse after verse, at least fifty in all. I just laid there mad, listening.

By the end of the tape, something began to happen. I remember a faith rising up from deep down inside my spirit, and I said out loud, "You know what, devil? I am about to get to know God in a way I would never have if this hadn't happened to me, so thank you!" I grabbed my Bible and rewound the tape to the beginning, highlighting in my Bible each verse that man quoted. When I got to the end of the tape again, I went back to Genesis and put a sticky tab on every page that had a highlighted verse. After that, I got up and began to limp in excruciating pain around my little, dingy apartment, reciting (or should I say yelling as loud as I could at God?) each one of those Scriptures, starting in Genesis.

I was in so much pain. I would yell, "God! You said! You said, 'By Your stripes, I'm healed,' Either You are who You say You are or You're not. Which is it? God, You said, 'I sent My word and healed them.'"

I cried out to the Lord, reciting each one of those verses to Him from Genesis to Revelation. Somewhere in the middle of the book of Psalms, I spotted out of the corner of my eye my pack of cigarettes on the counter. I yelled out, "Fine! I'll quit smoking!" I threw my package of cigarettes in the trash and kept yelling out verses to Him throughout the New Testament. "God, *you* said!" When I got through Revelation, I was done and worn out. I laid down on the floor, and I fell asleep. I don't know how long I was asleep, but when I woke up, I was completely healed. From the top of my head to the soles of my feet, the pain was completely *gone!* I also never had the desire for another cigarette another day in my life.

I will never, ever forget that day. The Holy Spirit walked me step-by-step on how to take Jesus at His Word and receive a miracle. I jumped up, leaping and rejoicing. I remember saying to My Savior that day, "You really are who You say You are. You do what You say You will do. I will go where You want me to go! You are mine, and I am Yours."

Luke's Gospel Chapter 7 talks about a sinful woman, forgiven of much, in verses 36-50. She found Jesus, washed His feet with her tears, and anointed them with fragrant oil. It was Jesus' mercy and goodness that motivated her deeply extravagant worship.

I had found the One I had been looking for all along.

I Will Go Where You Want Me to Go

It wasn't long after that I was getting ready to graduate from my two years of Bible School. I knew for sure that God was calling me to "Native American Ministry." So, I decided to google: Native American Ministry in Northern Arizona and NAOMI House was the only place that came up in my search.

This was when I showed up in Linda's office, circling back to Chapter 1.

I found my church home very soon after arriving in Northern Arizona, where I was 'adopted' by my Pastor, Jerry Keams. Our ministry partnership was a kingdom connection for sure.

Very soon after meeting him, he invited me to minister behind the pulpit. Something I had only done one other time in my life, but I knew deep down it was God calling me! I remember the very first message I preached behind his pulpit, "Children, obey your parents in the Lord," speaking of spiritual parents (pastors).

It wasn't until I stepped out in faith at NAOMI House that I realized I had a call and serious passion for teaching God's sharp and powerful word and preaching His Gospel.

Concluding Reflections

Preparing ourselves for the reality of kingdom service, being developed and discipled for the many battles we will find there is so important.

The truth is, God is calling His sons and daughters to the front in this hour. And if you're like me, there was a whole lot for me to heal from and to learn.

This next section talks about the pain and power in the preparation.

PART 2

━━━━━━━━⟶)•(⟵━━━━━━━━

Preparing for the Call

"You cannot be my disciple, unless you
love me more than you love
your father and mother, your wife and
children, and your brothers and sisters.
You cannot come with me unless you love
me more than you love your own life.
You cannot be my disciple unless you carry
your own cross and come with me.
Suppose one of you wants to build a tower.
What is the first thing you will do?
Won't you sit down and figure out how much it will cost
and if you have enough money to pay for it?"

~Luke 14:26-28 (CEV)~

9

Called to the Front

> "So, the last will be first, and the first last.
> For many are called, but few chosen."
>
> ~Matthew 20:16 (NKJV)~

I rushed into the Emergency Room in our small town on Christmas morning. My pastor's wife had called with deep distress in her voice: "Sister, it's not good. Pastor's not doing good." "I'm on my way," I responded.

Just two short months prior, we all learned that our beloved pastor Jerry was diagnosed with cancer. I do not have enough room in this book to speak of my love, honor, and respect for my pastor, my spiritual father. We had ministered side by side for over thirteen solid years. We were rocking and rolling, ready to see God move amongst the people! He was a kingdom-minded, humble man; he was a man of courageous prayer and deep worship. His expectation for good to reign, willingness to develop and train the next generation of leaders, and his vision of hope for his people were inspiring and empowering.

But here I was, walking into his hospital room, up to his bed, the bed on which laid my man of God, my spiritual father. If he had passed, it was merely moments ago. My mind was running wild as I was trying to make sense of what was happening. Doctors were not expecting him to live very long, true, but no one expected him to be gone so soon. Of course, we were all standing in prayer and agreement for a miracle healing from cancer, yet here I was.

As I walked slowly toward his shell of a body lying on the bed, I realized there were two people standing over him weeping—his son and his sister. The next thoughts happened in a matter of seconds. Honestly, my very first thought was to command him to come back to life in Jesus' Name! Immediately after that, my thought was, I don't want to offend the people standing here, his family members. And thirdly, my thought was, what if he doesn't want to come back?

It was as if I heard my pastor speak to me in his kind, fatherly voice: "Daughter, daughter." I saw him lovingly shush me, putting his hands up gently, saying: "Sister, I don't want to come back."

That was it. I knew that was it. I stood as close to his bedside as I could get as I realized he was standing in the very presence of His Father—his good, good Father. He was standing right in the glory of God that he and I had only preached about. My pastor was a general of the faith who carried an Apostolic mantle in this region. To say that his family, friends, the Body of Christ, and I all miss him terribly is surely an understatement. (see Photo #8 on page 243)

It wasn't until after his passing that the story of Elijah being caught up in a whirlwind and Elisha receiving the double-portion mantle brought a deeper meaning to me. The story is found in 2 Kings 2:9-13 (NKJV):

> And so it was, when they had
> crossed over, that Elijah said to Elisha,
> "Ask! What may I do for you, before I
> am taken away from you?" Elisha said,

"Please let a double portion of your spirit be upon me."

So, he said, "You have asked a hard thing. *Nevertheless, if you see me when I am taken from you, it shall be so for you*; but if not, it shall not be *so.*"

Then it happened, as they *continued on* and *talked,* that suddenly a chariot of fire *appeared* with horses of fire and *separated the two of them*; and Elijah *went up* by a whirlwind into heaven.

And *Elisha saw it, and* he cried out, "My father, my father, the chariot of Israel and its horsemen!" So, he saw him no more. And he took hold of his own clothes and tore them into two pieces.

He also *took up the mantle of Elijah that had fallen from him* and went back and stood by the bank of the Jordan."

While there may be other ways to interpret this passage, here is what the Lord spoke to me as I was standing next to my pastor's bedside that Christmas morning.

The reason Elijah told Elisha he was asking for a hard thing when asking for the double-portion anointing is found in verse 10: "You have asked a hard thing, because only the one who is found standing, remaining by my [Elijah's] side when I'm taken up, will be eligible for the double-portion anointing, and the mantle that will fall in that moment." The Message Version says: "That's a hard one!" said Elijah. "But if you're watching when I'm taken from you, you'll get what you've asked for. But only if you're watching."

Wow! What God spoke to my heart was this, "Daughter, it is not easy to stay connected with your leadership throughout the storms of life and ministry. Almost everything will try to get you to wander or quit. Nevertheless, those who are willing to remain, walking side-by-side in covenant, know this: When a mantle is being transferred, it will descend in a double-anointing measure, and you, and others, will grab that baton and run."

There will be plenty of times where you will feel seriously challenged just to stay connected to Father God and the truth of His Word when walking through the seasons of our Christian journey. But, because Elisha was paying attention because he determined to remain in close proximity moment by moment, season by season, he found himself in the right place at the right time. And when that double-portion anointing, that mantle fell from Elijah, he picked it up, put it on, and *the legacy continued.*

The Bible talks about a great cloud of witnesses in Hebrews 12:1 (NKJV):

> Since we are surrounded by so great a cloud of witnesses, let us lay aside every weight, and the sin which so easily ensnares us, and let us run with endurance the race that is set before us.

I personally believe my Pastor has taken his seat amongst the witnesses and is cheering us all on from glory.

You know what? It really does matter to whom you are connected—the decade, the era, the generation, the pastor, the leadership you are in covenant with *matter.* God is not playing Russian roulette with your life. Nobody said it would be easy. Many of our spiritual generals have gone on to be with the Lord, and the baton must be passed. The question that demands an answer is, are we ready to receive it?

The Need for Developing Leaders Today

Ministry can be defined: to meet a need. Ministry is simply acknowledging a need right in front of you and being willing to step in to respond to it. Sometimes, this happens with only a burden or a passion spurring you forward. There are many, many needs today, and the call for Native Christian leaders, as well as all Christian leaders, is more urgent now than ever before.

As it pertains to Native American ministry specifically, I offer the following excerpt taken directly out of teaching material provided by one of my spiritual fathers, apostle Fred Smith. Written in March of 2010, it is titled "The Native American Curse":

The blood of Native Americans cries out from the ground of all fifty states. Centuries ago, settlers were sent with an apostolic mandate to establish one nation under god. God never intended for the original inhabitants of the land to be crushed in order to fulfill His purpose. Nevertheless, a lust for land, gold, and power corrupted many settlers and, as a result, cost the lives of millions of Native Americans.

> ➤ Conservative historians indicate that 12–15 million Native Americans were murdered, which is twice the number of human lives taken during the holocaust.

- ➢ Biological warfare transmitting smallpox through blankets and clothing caused the disappearance of complete tribes forever.

- ➢ Over 500 treaties have been broken.

- ➢ The forced sterilization of Native American women was a form of genocide.

- ➢ Indian children were separated from family and placed in boarding schools where hundreds of documented cases were verifying sexual and physical abuse within these boarding schools.

- ➢ Alcoholism affects seventy-five percent of Native households.

- ➢ The American Indian average life expectancy is 40.9 for men and 46 years for women.

- ➢ The suicide rate for American Indians is five times higher than any other ethnic group.

- ➢ Teen suicide on reservations is three times higher than the national average.

- ➢ The school dropout rate is three times higher than the national average.

- ➢ The infant mortality rate is two times higher than the national average.

Do we really have the luxury of turning our heads in the other direction?

Matthew 20:16 says, "The last will be first, and the first last. For many are called, but few chosen." This means many are invited to come into partnership with God's will and plans for their lives, but few will respond to that invitation. As well, it is even harder to remain over time. Why? Luke 14:26-28 tells us to "count the cost" when it comes to following Jesus. Verse 26 reads, "if anyone comes to Me and does not hate his father and mother, wife and children, brothers and sisters, yes, and his own life also, he cannot be My disciple."

Ouch, that's pretty harsh. He is saying if you do not love Him and His path for you more than family, self, or anything else for that matter, it will be impossible to fully follow Him. Verse 27 declares, "And whoever does not bear his cross and come after Me cannot be My disciple."

Have you noticed we really don't hear much about living the *crucified life,* the total surrender to God, His Word, and His ways? Verse 28 asks, "for which of you, intending to build a tower, does not sit down first and *count the cost,* whether he has enough to finish it?" It is quite easy to get excited about a calling in our life. It can be exhilarating even to be passionate about something like advancing God's kingdom. However, when the emotion wears off and you are left with the harsh reality of the life of a *servant,* will we have the commitment and perseverance to see it through and finish strong? Matthew 20:26-27 (NKJV) notes, "But whosoever desires to become great among you, let him be your servant. And whoever desires to be first among you, let him be your slave."

I will never forget those first few weeks after packing up my life in Phoenix and moving to NAOMI House to respond to God's call to ministry. There I was, Exit 269, basically in the middle of nowhere, the desert. I always say, in order to put it in perspective, we are 70 miles from the nearest Starbucks!

All I had was a word from the Lord to *go!* I remember I was sitting in one of our buildings, looking out the window at the tumbleweeds blowing in the wind. There was nothing but I-40 Highway and train tracks heading East and West for miles and miles and miles.

I have to tell you it was hard. I looked out that window in silence, but really I was crying out as loud as I could on the inside: *"God!* I thought You loved me. I thought You had great plans for my life! Did I hear You correctly? Was I really supposed to step out like this and follow You?" And guess what? I had many, many more times of crying out like that.

Ministry can be hard! Responding in faith isn't always easy. There is really no sugar-coating ministry. Yes! There are certainly highs, victories, and times of breakthrough and the miraculous. But I'm talking about the long hours and days in between—feeling overworked, underpaid, and underappreciated as the days, weeks and months roll on. Maybe you have, or maybe you just might find yourself in a place of sincerely questioning God's character while walking out your calling. Are You really good? All the time? Are You really trustworthy? Are You really reliable, dependable, and present? Are You going to see me through? You fill in the blank. Don't we all have a list of non-stop questions for God? You will come to find out that, like me, it was *never* God's character that was in question or being tested. It was *mine.*

The Necessity of Character

Character implies an unwavering dedication to a set of standards. It speaks of walking above the average mark or in excellence. Character means integrity—the ability to harmoniously integrate our words and our actions so the gap between the two narrows.

God is undivided. He is the same yesterday, today, and forever. That is why you can trust Him. To be a person of character means we are trustworthy, reliable, and dependable. It is to have a commitment to a set of values that you will not compromise regardless of the circumstance, pressure, or situation.

Somebody says, "Process!" Someone with character carefully welcomes and adheres to accountability. They are disciplined to self-regulate for the sake of moral convictions—commitment, dedication, integrity, sacrifice, discipline, conformity to standards, and so forth. All these represent characteristics of strong character. And these are all developed as a process over time through the storms and seasons of our life.

I remember years ago, a mentor of mine saying: "Honey, your call can never take you where your character can't keep you." I have never forgotten those wise words. They seared my heart and soul as the Lord let the weight of this truth make a lasting impression upon my life.

The following is a quote regarding the making of a leader from a spiritual father:

> We must take a good look at character deficiencies, hidden sin, and reasons as to why we are tested. We need to learn

how to deal with being misunderstood, falsely accused, what to do when everything goes the opposite direction of our heartfelt prayers, and believing God for breakthroughs. Learning how to handle frustration, what to do when we walk through seasons of dryness, barrenness, or coldness, are imperative. We must gain an understanding of what it means to be 'forged in the fire and finished in the flame.' God is forming and fashioning us after His likeness and His image, all the while He is providing us with everything we need to be successful on the journey. His grace, His mercies, His integrity, all are working in us to accomplish all that He has started.

Job 23:10 (NKJV) summarizes, "But He knows the way I take; when He has tested me, I shall come forth as gold." There is an urgent call to the Body of Christ in this generation to rise to the mandate of *becoming leaders*, that is, spiritual mothers and fathers. First Corinthians 4:15 says we have many instructors in Christ, yet not many fathers.

The Warrior Spirit Within Must Be Developed

Second Timothy 2:20-21 (NKJV) claims:

> In a great house there are not only vessels of gold and silver, but also of wood and clay, some for honor and some for

dishonor. Therefore, if anyone cleanses himself from these things [who separates himself from contact with the contaminating and corrupting influences], he will be a vessel for honor, sanctified set apart for a special purpose and], useful and profitable to the Master, *prepared* for every good work.

The Message version translates verse 21 this way, "Become the kind of container God can use to present any and every kind of gift to his guests for their blessing."

The price to respond to His calling includes picking up your cross and counting the cost. The God-given warrior spirit must become submitted to the preparation process. "Prepared" means to be made ready for specific use through necessary preparations. That process can be painful at times. Between the beginning and the end product of what God is accomplishing in and through you is sometimes called the wilderness. Being in the wilderness can be very lonely. You can feel isolated, rejected, undervalued, and even forsaken.

But realize being in the wilderness is just the process, not the end result. There are things in this middle phase that God is working in you that *will enable you to be able to withstand underneath the weight of the promise fulfilled.*

Never forget this! The reward will far outweigh the pain of development. Paul suffered tremendously for the sake of the Gospel, but his conviction was this: "for I consider that the sufferings of this present life are not worthy to be compared with the glory that is about to be revealed to us and in us" (Romans 8:18). Paul took an inventory of all the persecutions, afflictions, the thorn in his flesh, hardships, abuses, mistreatments, and spiritual warfare and came to this conclusion—*none* of it is worthy to be compared to the glory that is coming. The Passion version concludes, "I'm convinced that these things are less than nothing compared to the magnitude of glory that is about to be unveiled in us."

Take a look around; what is the most difficult circumstance you are currently facing? When you look at the sting of rejection, or the loneliness of being shunned, or the difficulties of persecution you may be facing, like Paul, you must realize there is really no comparison to what God is going to unveil in you. What is He going to unveil? It's not *what,* but *who*—Himself!

God wants to unveil Himself through me and you to this generation. As Romans 8:19 (NKJV) reads, "for [even the whole] creation waits expectantly and longs earnestly for God's sons to be made known [waits for the revealing, the disclosing of their sonship]." The whole earth, our children, the unsaved, those we are assigned to are all literally groaning, earnestly waiting with expectation for God to "show who His children are." They will be known and recognized as His children, those who are led by the Spirit of God (Romans 8:14, NKJV).

In sum, learning how to be led by the Spirit of God is a process. It is a process of preparation. And time spent in preparation *is never wasted time.*

God Has a Specific Plan for Every Person

Jeremiah 1:5 (AMPC) claims:

> Before I formed you in the womb,
> I knew [and] approved of you [as My
> chosen instrument], and before you were

born, I separated and set you apart, con-
secrating you; [and] I appointed you as a
prophet to the nations.

God had a plan for Jeremiah even before he was born. Each one of us was born with a purpose. God's desire is that we live for Him and allow Him to fulfill His plan in us. Romans 11:29 (AMP) reads:

For the gifts and callings of God are irrevocable. [He never withdraws them when once they are given, and He does not change His mind about those to whom he gives His grace or to whom He sends His call.

Everything God created was created to *solve a problem.* Do you know what that means? You are a walking solution for somebody, for some situation, for some need. Somebody needs exactly what *you* have been given by God.

It is our responsibility to discover our calling by seeking God, trusting Him, obeying Him, and responding to a need that is right in front of us. We who compose the Body of Christ are being called upon by God to meet these needs. God's peace, provision, power, and prosperity are wrapped up in our total surrender to fulfill our calling.

Jeremiah 29:11-14 (MSG) declares:

For I know the thoughts, plans and purposes that I think toward you, says the Lord, thoughts of peace and not of evil, to give you a future and a hope. Then

you will call upon Me and go and pray to
Me, and I will listen to you. And you will
seek Me and find Me, when you search
for Me *with all your heart*. Yes, when you
get serious about finding me and want it
more than anything else, I'll make sure
you won't be disappointed.

The word "seek" in this verse is used at least 244 times
in the Old Testament, having three definitions:

1.   *"baqash"*—to search out by any method, but spe-
     cifically in worship and prayer. It implies to strive
     after by begging, asking, or desire;
2.   *"darash"*—to tread or frequent a place, to follow,
     pursue; practice and study; and
3.   *"shachar"*—to dawn; to search for or enquire painstak-
     ingly and diligently, specifically early in the morning.

Most people really don't feel adequate to respond to
God. You don't have to think very hard to come up with a list
of excuses/reasons as to why we reject or put off God's nudge
to respond to His call upon our lives. Maybe you can relate
to one or more in this list of common excuses:

1.   Plain and simple, I just don't feel like it, or I don't
     want to.
2.   I do not feel adequate or qualified, or I do not
     know how.
3.   It's inconvenient, or the timing is wrong.
4.   There is no one to help or mentor me.
5.   This doesn't really fit in with the plans I have for
     my life right now.

6. Giving my life over to the Lord in order to respond to His calling is going to be too difficult. This sounds painful.
7. I'm scared.

Matthew 14:27-31 (NKJV) describes how the disciples were out on the water in their comfortable boat when they saw something walking on water, and they became scared.

> Immediately Jesus spoke to them, saying, "Be of good cheer! It is I. Do not be afraid." And Peter answered Him and said, "Lord, if it is You, command me to come to You on the water." So He said, "Come." And when Peter had come down out of the boat, he walked on the water to go to Jesus. But when he saw that the wind was boisterous, *he was afraid;* and beginning to sink he cried out, saying, "Lord, save me!" And immediately Jesus stretched out His hand and caught him, and said to him, "O you of little faith, why did you doubt?"

The truth is that no one ever accomplished anything of significance in this life who wasn't willing to step out of the boat, even on nothing but a nudge, a hunch, a feeling, or sensing. One pastor of mine said, "You'll just know it in your knower." We simply must refuse to live our lives in fear of stepping out into our God-given destiny. Or, like Joyce Meyer says, "Do it afraid."

Maybe you wish you had a mentor or a teacher, someone to show you how. But what if God wants to raise *you* up as the spiritual father or mother? For many? God rarely consults us to inquire if it is a convenient time to give Him our "yes." Maybe you simply *don't want* to respond to a need. If not you, who? If not now, when? Luke concludes, "All who are obsessed with being secure in life will lose it all—including their lives. But those who let go of their lives and surrender them to Me will discover true life" (Luke 17:33, TPT).

All of creation is awaiting God's glory being revealed through you. God does not call the qualified. He qualifies those whom He calls and who respond in availability. Like the story of Elisha and the widow's oil (2 Kings 4), as long as there were empty vessels, the supernatural oil, the empowerment of the Holy Spirit, was poured out. There is something supernatural that happens when you give God your "yes." He comes to empower us to accomplish what we could never do on our own. One of my favorite quotes puts it this way: "Faith is standing on the side of the mountain and taking a step knowing that He will either move the mountain under my feet, or He will teach me how to fly."

Even as it pertains to writing and releasing this book, I gave God my yes, and then I was faced with some extreme circumstances that made me want to back down. I had to repeatedly resist the urge to quit. God could have easily used somebody else, and believe me, I provided Him with an endless list of reasons as to why I concluded He had chosen the wrong person.

I eventually had to come to a decision, step out in faith and simply choose to trust Him with all of the many questions in my heart. I said, "God, I believe You asked me to do this, so I give you my, yes, and I know You will do the rest.

I don't know what God has set in front of you, but my prayer is that our hearts' response be this: "Today, I have decided to move forward in God."

We are all called to do something. You and I are all called to fulfill a purpose, to reach a destiny, to be all that God created us to be, and to do all that God created us to do. Our calling is that God-given passion that can never be quenched, that assignment we were born to fulfill.

Listen, I feel just as unqualified as the next guy! Don't we all feel that way when God calls us to do something? Whether it's to launch an outreach, or create a Facebook ministry page, and go *live* with this Gospel message, or write a book! The Christian life is never boring. Serving others, making commitments, giving God our yes is risky, and often times we hold back. Why? Because we don't feel empowered. We don't feel qualified. When it comes to our obedience to His nudges, we often spend our time looking to "self" rather than to Christ and His ability. We look at what we don't have and where we are lacking, whether that be education, influence, finances, wisdom, or courage.

Don't we feel like Moses? God spoke to Him radically, right out of a burning bush, declaring he shall go to Pharaoh—and speak for Yahweh! Moses' response was like you and me. "But God. I am not eloquent; I am slow of speech. Please send someone else." I know that's how I tend to sound. God no, please. Not me. I'm afraid. I'm weak. I'm incapable and unqualified. I. Am. Not. Enough.

I love what He told Moses when asked: "Lord, whom shall I say sent me?" He said, "Tell them I Am Who I Am has sent me to you" (Exodus 3:14, NKJV). Read that again.

God is looking for those who will arise in courage and faith. Not in themselves, but in Him. And if we are honest, there is something hard-wired on the inside of us that yearns to do just that. We were created to live bold, brave, daring and confident, in Him—even in the face of continual adversity. God has called us to enforce His finished work. God has called us as resilient warriors. To respond to this innate desire to live bold for Him and His Glory is to truly live.

Concluding Reflections

Responding in faith to God's call is our responsibility.

While we are on our journey to help meet the needs of others and introduce them to the Healer, you might discover, like me, it was you who needed the healing.

Let's talk about inner healing for the wounded warrior.

Word of the Lord through Genevieve, February 2006

> I am searching, yes, I am searching for a generation that is willing to be tested, purified, proven, and transformed—a generation ready to be renewed. I am searching because my people are perishing. Jesus says, come to Him, and He will give you rest. Whatever you need, you can have it in abundance. Anything that you ask, you can have it, according to His will. Just come without reservation.
>
> Why do you wait? Why do you wait? I Am ready. You keep asking, and I keep giving. Why? Because I already gave it to you. Prostrate yourself, be purified so that together we can prove to this dying world the good, acceptable, and perfect will of My Father. It is My perfect

will that all come to know and desire Me. It is My perfect will that all be healed, delivered, and restored by Me. But why would they come to Me when you have so perversely represented Me as a God who doesn't care? As a God who is many light years away? As a God who is incapable and unreachable?

Your religion and doctrines are perverse to Me. Why do you try so hard on your own? I already did that part when I took the keys. I already did all the hard work that you needlessly toil with. It is done! You are not inventing something new on your own. It has already been established. Please, sit back and let me be God. Please, just trust Me and obey Me so that I can prove to be God not only for your benefit but on behalf of the human race, whom I created and love.

You are Mine! I have bought you with a price. Repent, son of man, repent, child of God, repent, Christian. And then I will forgive you for not letting me transform you for the sake of the kingdom. The sacrifice is never greater than the reward, but you have to trust Me. Do you trust Me?

You will be judged for your lack of faith and trust. There is a time to pluck out and a time to plant, a time to destroy, and a time to be built up. Let me do it My way. Trust Me that I will build you up. Nothing is impossible for Me. I will heal you completely—mind, body, and spirit. Nothing will be missing. You are not waiting on Me. I am waiting on you. "Draw nigh unto Me and let Me be God. I will do the work—you just do what I ask you to do today," says the Lord.

10

The Necessity of
Inner Healing

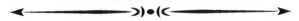

"Yea, I have loved thee with an everlasting love;
therefore, with loving kindness have I drawn thee.
Again, I will restore thee, and thou shalt be built."

~Jeremiah 31:2-4 (KJV)~

I found myself writhing on the floor in a fetal position as if I
were in pain. The visiting evangelist, a woman from Detroit,
had just laid hands on me in prayer. I went flying backward
and was thrown to the ground under the power of the Holy
Spirit.

The evangelist was preaching the Gospel in my church
that morning. She stood behind the pulpit and read passage
after passage of Jesus making circuits throughout regions
"preaching the Gospel" and "healing the sick." When her
time was up, she declared, "Let's pray and see what the Holy
Spirit would want to do."

She came walking through the crowd and began praying for healings and miracles over the people. As she made
her way down the aisle of my little church in Phoenix, she
glanced to her right where my sister and I were sitting. She
pointed her finger right at us and said: "You two! Come out
here."

My sister and I were brand new Christians. I was simply on fire for the Lord, filled with the Holy Ghost, and read my Bible every day. I wanted all that He had for me, and I knew there were areas of my life that needed His power. She was praying for people for physical healing, but I couldn't think of a physical need that I had at that moment.

My sister was first. She said, "What do you need from the Lord?" My sister mentioned she had asthma. The evangelist declared: "Oh, asthma is so easy for God. She prayed and laid hands on her, and my sister was out on the floor under the power of God.

It was my turn. She turned and said: "And you? What do you need from the Lord?" I admitted there wasn't a physical need I could think of but that I believed I needed a lot of help in my emotions. I didn't say much more than that, and she laid her hands on me, and I flew backward. As I was manifesting on the floor under the power of God, I heard a blood-curdling scream come out from deep down in my guts. It came barreling up throughout my body and out my mouth. The "loin-clothe ushers" were scurrying around in a frenzy at the commotion. The evangelist yelled out: "Leave her alone! God is working on her!" as she continued to pray for the people.

I experienced real deliverance that day from demonic oppression in my soul. Some would possibly feel embarrassed by such a scene. Not me. I was eternally grateful that the God that I had chosen to pursue with everything within me was truly powerful. The Jesus I read about in the Bible really is the same yesterday, today, and forever. God rescued me out of a deep, dark place. If the choice was my deliverance or my dignity, there was absolutely *no* contest.

At the point of my conversion, I cried out to God, "Send me! I'll go! What plans do you have for me? What am I to do for you on this earth? Anything! Have Your way in me!" I remember hearing Him respond, "Enroll in the Church's Bible school for two years, and then come talk to Me." I knew what He meant. He was saying, "We have some work to do, daughter. There has been some damage done to your heart, some trauma that you have experienced. Together, you and I are going to walk through some much-needed healing."

I was a wounded warrior in pursuit of transformation through His Word and power. Isaiah 61:1 declares that part of Jesus' ministry is to *bind up* the brokenhearted. Literally translated, this means to heal the fragmented soul—the soul that has been broken, busted, fractured, shattered, or smashed into pieces. That was me!

The soul is the seat of the inner person where deeply embedded thought patterns, mindsets, belief systems, memories, appetites, emotions, passions, and desires dwell. This is why it can sometimes take so long to be free. The Good News is, Jesus is the Great Physician, and the Holy Spirit is the Great Psychiatrist. There is *no* sin, trauma, bloodline iniquity, abuse, transgression, or darkness in any part of our soul that is too strong for the Light of the Truth!

> *Restoration* means to bring back to a former condition, to an unimpaired and improved condition. To reconstruct; it is acquiring a replacement story.

Even with a clear call of God on your life, frontline ministry can be the toughest kind of work there is. When our hearts truly cry, *"Thy Kingdom come! Thy will be done in the earth as it is in Heaven"* (Matthew 6:10, KJV), realize His kingdom must be *first* established in us.

Let's be clear. The enemy isn't too concerned about people who will do no more than warm a church pew. However, he is greatly concerned, and should be, about a person, a family, or a people who will take their rightful position as kings and priests, carrying and heralding the good news of the kingdom!

Stepping into your God-given assignment usually means entering into unchartered territory *in you and* around you. Everything in your life will be put to the test. That includes your mind, will, and emotions (the soul), your marriage, children and family, your finances and health; it will include your belief systems and cultural views. *All* of these will be *tested!* That is why in 2 Timothy 2:3-5 (NKJV), Paul admonished the younger minister Timothy:

> You, therefore, must endure hardship as a good soldier of Jesus Christ. No one engaged in warfare entangles himself with the affairs of *this* life, that he may please him who enlisted him as a soldier. And also, if anyone competes in athletics, he is not crowned unless he competes according to the rules.

Above All Else, Guard Your Heart

After our initial salvation experience, our soul must be *immersed* in His presence and cautiously maintained, protected, and nourished by His Word. If we fail to do this, we can become an easy target for the enemy, providing an open door or a legal landing strip on our wounded soul. This is how so many people are "taken out" of their God-given assignments.

Proverbs 4:23 (NLT) warns, "Guard your heart above all else, with all vigilance and above all that your guard, for it determines the course of your life." The word *heart* in this verse is not an organ that pumps blood. Rather, it is the Hebrew word *lav,* which is translated as "the soul," meaning your mind, will, and emotions. Our thoughts, feelings, and decisions.

The CEB translation counsels, "More than anything you guard, protect your mind, for life flows from it." The CJB translation instructs, "Above everything else, guard your soul; for it is the source of life's consequences." The DRA translation advises, "With all watchfulness keep your soul, because life issues out from it." You get my point?

Why does the Bible put such great emphasis on guarding your soul? Because the enemy is looking for any open door to access a believer's life so that he can wear us down or discredit us. His ultimate purpose is to cause us to cease to operate in our calling.

Notice whose responsibility it is to guard your heart. *Ours!* The truth is, *if we don't like the quality of our life, it is a direct result of the condition of our soul.* As ambassadors, representatives, ministers of reconciliation, *sent ones*; this is so vitally important to realize because ministry can be messy! Ministry can be traumatic! For example, ministry pertaining to children's homes or foster care can be very traumatic. Second-hand trauma is real, and therefore the well-being of one's soul is utterly important.

Anyone called to ministry can tell you that ministry trauma can be painful and difficult. How about church-hurt? Ouch! Many people have learned these things the hard way. When you give God your "yes," you are positioned for some of the greatest miracles of heaven as well as some of the fiercest schemes the enemy utilizes. You enter into territory that is currently occupied by the enemy who has no intention to relinquish ground or the souls of the occupants.

The battle is for the souls of this generation, and the enemy sees you as a threat to his dominion and goals. Therefore, you will be squeezed, probed, analyzed, sifted, and studied for the purpose of finding any possible, or perhaps many possible, openings in your life.

In Luke 22:31-32a, Jesus explained to Simon Peter Satans' desire to sift him like wheat and test his faith. It reads like this in The Passion Version:

> "Peter, my dear friend, listen to what I'm about to tell you. Satan has obtained permission to come and sift you all like wheat and test your faith. But I have prayed for you, Peter, that you would stay faithful to me no matter what comes…"

You will have ample opportunity for accusations, offenses, and attacks. Therefore, your soul must be systematically renewed daily (Romans 12:2). The reality of experiencing fatigue and exhaustion is real, and you will have no choice but to intentionally guard your soul. This is foundational to understand for those who know they have been called to serve people in God's name.

For example, I was not aware, on a conscious level, that by saying a loud yes to serve the beautiful children at NAOMI House, I was also declaring a loud "no" to the orphan spirit hovering over a territory. Simply by responding to God's call and stepping into my assignment, by itself, was essentially declaring war on such evils as abandonment, rejection, and generational trauma. Just to name a few.

I didn't recognize this at first, but it became abundantly clear over some time that I would need my own healing in the exact places where I was called to confront. In my own life, the pangs of rejection and abandonment had set up camp in the orphaned child in me, fragmenting my soul.

The ministry has a way of probing you and squeezing you to the point that whatever is in you will come out of you. Just like squeezing a tube of toothpaste. What's on the inside will simply spill over. The good, the bad, and the ugly. This is true for each one of us. When we come into the high stresses of ministry and spiritual warfare, what is truly on the inside begins to "manifest." This is why many people will end up quitting too soon. We step out in faith, we get squeezed, and we are subsequently confronted with the dilemma of the catastrophic disconnect between who we are called to be in Christ and who we are currently while in the process of sanctification and growth.

It can be quite a devastating experience when we are forced to come face to face with ourselves! Many people will simply take the pressure off by waving the white flag and retreating to a "regular" life.

For those who stick it out, we can easily revert to human nature and its' desire to blame something/anything on the outside of us for what is coming up from *within* us. However, the truth is this; if *it* were never in you, *it* would never come out of you.

Healing for the fragmented soul has to be an ongoing pursuit for every believer, and there is truly no one else responsible for that process, then ourselves.

There simply must be *deliverance for the deliverer*.

Deliverance for the Deliverer

An encounter of salvation in Christ can happen in a moment's time. At the very moment, we put our faith in the finished work of the cross and receive the precious gift in Christ's blood. Our spirit is instantaneously made perfect. However, our soul, the condition of our mind (thoughts), will (decisions), and emotions (feelings) must undergo a progressive transformation (Romans 12:2), deliverance, and renewal, from glory to glory (2 Corinthians 3:18).

It's one thing to suffer in your soul as a sinner separated from God, but what about when you have entered the family of God, and your soul is still damaged? I mean, you know you're going to heaven, praise God, but what about the negative mindsets, memories, belief systems, and old habits that still linger? This is why people, even believers in the church, can be saved and sick, saved and depressed, saved and addicted, saved and angry, saved and making destructive decisions, and so on.

When I first became a Christian, I had a pastor whom I highly looked up to. He and his beautiful wife were powerfully anointed by God. Their teaching and preaching ministry trained me in many beneficial ways. Unfortunately, this pastor decided to entertain the dark corners of his soul and ultimately ended up going to prison for inappropriate online behavior with minors. This was my introduction to the fact that you can operate in a God-given gift and at the same time be living in habitual and willful sin. That is until it catches up with you. You really cannot assume someone's character based upon their charisma or giftings. Sadly, this reality has manifested itself throughout my ministry experience in countless ways. In fact, none of us are impervious to the enemy's schemes. These harsh statistics in the body of

Christ have deeply impacted me by inspiring Holy, reverential fear over my own life. We simply must take responsibility. Truly, we have no power to change those around us. Not your spouse, not your leaders, not anyone. We will only be accountable for our own hearts and lives as we walk before the Lord.

One thing I want to point out about this couple I just mentioned is that his wife went on to be and do all that God had called her to regardless of his decisions. She wrote a book about it, which I recommend. Her book addresses things like pornography in the church and much more.[6] Sadly, these types of moral failures in leadership are all too common. Again, the enemy would love for every Christian to think that to follow Christ is to simply repeat a sinners' prayer. He would love for us to be deceived into thinking lukewarm living is good enough. To be honest, lukewarm is the perfect temperature for the works of the flesh and demonic activity to comfortably persist!

I will mention another couple, who were married and getting ready to be used mightily by God when it was discovered, unbeknownst to the wife, that the husband had been molesting children almost all of his adult life, including during his pastoral ministry. The wife in this scenario is the founder of NAOMI House. A very long and powerful story later, Linda went on to fulfill God's calling upon her life, and out of the very ashes of her devastation, NAOMI House was born.

God is the God of restoration!

There have been many times throughout my years of ministry that I have had to learn to *lead with a limp*. God has a way of working every tragedy and trauma of our past, present, or future together for your good and His glory if *you* walk upright before the Lord.

Bad things happen, even to good people. Regardless of the carelessness or reckless decisions that others make, we must learn to trust Him at every turn and continue to keep our eyes fixed on Him through it all.

No Dark Corners

Truthfully, not one of us is exempt from our enemy who prowls and looks for someone to devour (1 Peter 5:8). Members of the Church, including clergy, are certainly not exempt from the devastation of deeply-rooted strongholds.

I know of countless other stories of ministry casualties that aren't as visible but just as devastating nonetheless. Whether it was through spirits of addiction, alcohol, lust, greed, or any other myriad of life-controlling issues, many have not been able to complete their mission simply because of the dark parts of the soul that were never exposed, surrendered, and delivered.

In fact, could it be that we, as men and women called to do mighty things for God, are specific targets? I say that not to scare you. But only to admonish us all. We must make a daily choice to give up the dark parts of our lives, to let more and more of His light and love shine in. We must choose to live *all out* for Him. We cannot be delivered from that which we entertain. And we lose the authority to confront that which we have in common (John 14:30, AMP).

It is possible to allow darkness to gain access and a foothold in areas of our lives that we haven't completely surrendered to the Lord or to the Light. Luke 11:36 (NLT) puts it like this:

> If you are filled with light, *with no dark corners,* then your whole life will be radiant, as though a floodlight were filling you with light.

Dark corners or the dark parts are those areas of our lives that we haven't completely surrendered to the Lord.

God has called you and me out of darkness and into the marvelous light (1 Peter 2:9). He gave us His word to light the way (Psalm 119:105). The Word of God is the light, and it exposes us. *Don't run from it, run to it!*

One of my spiritual fathers captures it this way: "The same anointing that exposes and reveals you is the same anointing that heals, delivers, and sets you free." Do not allow pride or a lackadaisical attitude to keep you from being *totally* free in your mind, will, or emotions. The price is too high.

God looks at our hearts on an individual basis. As ministers and ambassadors of heaven, we must adopt the prayer of David found in Psalm 139:23-24:

> "Search me, O God, and know my heart; Try me, and know my anxieties; and see if there is any wicked way in me, and lead me in the way everlasting."

I am reminded of an old-school gospel song that says: "It's me. It's me. It's me, O Lord. Standing in the need of prayer."

Instead of giving in to guilt, shame, fear, impurity, and condemnation, instead of covering over or hiding our transgressions, we must allow desperation to drive us to a place in His presence that cannot be found any other way.

From Glory to Glory

Certainly, there are times of instant deliverance from the Lord, but for the most part, it will require systematically renewing the mind and encountering His presence *intentionally* and *regularly*. We must come diligently and continually to this *secret place*, drawing near to receive strength and empowerment from Him.

Those who name Jesus as Lord are being sent out with the ministry of reconciliation and have the mandate to dwell *in* Him. We *must* maintain a lifestyle of proximity, nearness, and closeness to God. As the created, we were made to live in the presence of the Creator. Apart from Him, we can do absolutely nothing that remains eternally (John 15:5).

We are to live and remain in proximity to His presence and heavenly atmosphere. "He that dwelleth in the secret place of The Most High shall abide under the shadow of the Almighty" (Psalm 91:1, KJV). In order to be under the shadow of something or someone, you have to be and stay close! We have to desire no distance between us.

Developing a deeply intimate walk with the Lord requires a predetermined mindset that will allow nothing to come in between my dwelling in Him.

> ➤ If sin causes distance, I don't want it.

> ➤ If unforgiveness, bitterness, or any other work of the flesh causes distance, I don't want it.

> ➤ If religion causes distance, I don't want it.

> ➤ If being busy serving and working for God is costing me my time with God, I don't want it.

> ➤ If distractions, relationships, my own insecurities, ignorance, attitude, or anything at all is causing distance, I don't want it.

We cannot earn nearness to God. That bill was graciously paid in full through the precious blood of Jesus (Ephesians 2:8-10). However, living in His nearness is much more than "repeat this prayer after me" salvation. It's a lifestyle of hunger and desperation for Him.

Hunger and desperation like that of brother Bartimaeus.

Jesus! Son of David! Have Mercy On ME!

I love the story of blind Bartimaeus in Mark 10. As he was sitting by the roadside begging, he heard that Jesus of Nazareth was passing by. He began to cry out loudly, "Jesus! Son of David! Have mercy on me!" All those around him tried to get him to be quiet, "Hush, keep it down." But he cried out all the louder, "Jesus! Son of David! Have mercy on me!" The Bible says that Jesus stood still and called him to Himself. Jesus said, "What do you want me to do for you?" Bartimaeus said, "That I may receive my sight." Jesus replied, "Your faith has made you well."

Brother Bartimaeus offers us a clue as to how to get a hold of the miracle-working power of God—desperation and a genuine encounter. These two things are often missing in the American church today. The opposite of true desperation is a mentality that is one foot in and one foot out, or complacent and unchallenged. Many times, the dark parts of the human soul go undisputed in our churches. These dark areas can remain quite comfortable on our cushioned pews of the status quo. The word "blind" in this passage means mentally blind or *blindness of soul;* darkened by cloudy, foggy smoke or to be wrapped in a mist; to make proud or puffed up with pride.

True desperation implies humility, and humility is a key that opens up the realm to the miraculous. This is why the enemy absolutely loves the devastating effects of pride in the believer's life. It is a direct hindrance to breakthroughs. Blind Bartimaeus' cry caught Jesus' attention. He was loud, persistent, and undignified. Where there is true desperation, there is an encounter. Where there is an encounter, there is a collision with miraculous deliverance. "Where the spirit of the Lord is, there is liberty." If that sounds familiar, it's because that's from 2 Corinthians 3:17.

Concluding Thoughts

1. At the very moment we ask Christ into our heart, our spirit man is made 100 percent new and perfect.
2. Abiding in Christ is what will produce fruitfulness in our lives, as His unique giftings and qualities that *were imparted to us before time start to reveal themselves.*

3. When we experience His presence, when we encounter Him, it will bring to life that which is dead and *unlock that which is lying dormant.* The opened Destiny Books of Heaven will reveal our assignments, which were written before the foundations of the world. *This is true for individuals, families as well as nations.*

4. As we determine to guard our hearts and lay our lives open for the light of God's truth to transform us inwardly and deeply, a flow of God's Spirit can flow freely through us, outwardly.

Tools that will enable us to walk according to the power of the Holy Spirit are what we will look at in this next chapter.

11

Thy Kingdom Come

←————————————➤)●(←————————————→

"Your kingdom come.
Your will be done on earth as it is in heaven."

~Matthew 6:10 (NKJV)~

The kingdom is ever-increasing (Isaiah 9:7), and there is absolutely no shortage in heaven. When God calls you into a destitute, dry land or tough ministry assignment, such as a reservation, keep in mind it's not random. Our reservations are simply *on reserve* for a coming outpouring of God's Glory like never seen before on earth. He needs sons and daughters who will hear His instructions, obey, and take the kingdom of heaven into places where they have been sent.

The Church or the *ecclesia* means "the called-out ones." It is the embassy of heaven on the earth. It is where we are to receive marching orders and be equipped to advance the heavens' agenda. As believers, we are being called upon for such a time as this. With the powers of darkness yelling so loudly, we cannot afford to remain silent.

Sometimes I wonder has the church, at large, been lullabied to sleep? Are we on autopilot, coasting down the lazy river of the lukewarm, bless-me-club and called it Christianity? We might hashtag it, quote it, and Instagram-post it, we might even highlight it on our Kindle. But if after that we are rolling over to hit the snooze button, then *we might be the very ones who have been anesthetized by the poison-tipped arrows of mediocrity.*

Every believer is being called upon as kingdom Enforcers. It is time for the Body of Christ to push back every opposing force from our seated position—in Christ from the third heaven. Our mentality must shift from a "Hang on until the sweet by and by" to "It ain't over" and "Not on my watch." Each of us must "find our Tribe" (our assigned jurisdiction), put our feet on the soil, and declare, "Thy Kingdom come (here), thy will be done [here]!"

We are Enforcers of Christ's Victory

We have been given the keys of the Kingdom of Heaven, the delegated authority to bind and loose or allow and disallow, according to what is already permitted or prohibited in heaven.

Matthew 16:19 (AMP) reads:

> I will give you the keys of the Kingdom of Heaven; and whatever you bind [declare to be improper and unlawful] on earth must be what is already bound in heaven; and whatever you lose [declare lawful] on earth must be what is already loosed in heaven.

If this is the case, it becomes imperative to know what is lawful or unlawful in heaven if we are going to go about binding and loosing, right?

I think we can all agree there is no sickness or disease in heaven. There are no evil statistics in heaven, no curses, no mental strongholds. Neither is their lack of any kind—no stress, no strife, no fear, etc. We do not need to execute healing, deliverance, financial assistance, or peace in heaven. We need those things released into our everyday lives, communities, families, and so on.

We must take a 360 degree look around the perimeter of our designated realms of influence and determine what is unlawful, what is out of alignment with heaven, and refuse to make peace with it. The holy Word of God, the Bible, is an official edict, a lawful decree of our covenant rights. Jesus came to give an abundant, uncommon, superior kind of life (John 10:10), and we must actively refuse to settle for less than our God-given inheritance and all that He died for.

The Ability to Dream Again

What is a curse? A curse is a concentrated spiritual force used by the enemy to sabotage the success and future of individuals, families, or nations. When left undealt with generation after generation, strongholds become reinforced over a place through the deeply embedded mindsets of the people. These mindsets create lifestyles or cycles of bondage.

When cycles of bondage are at work, people begin to accept the problems they face in their lives as *normal. This is just how it is.* What they fail to realize is the spiritual root of its origin.

This oversight often causes entire regions to live in a state of perpetual failure and defeat, having lost all expectation or hope for anything good. Proverbs 13:12 tells us the effect of facing disappointment after disappointment: "Hope deferred makes the heart sick. But when the desire [longing of one's heart; the dream] is fulfilled, it is a life-giving tree."

o Hope—an expectation of something good. Having a core belief system, trust, or belief in good.
o Deferred—delayed; to draw out, seize, prolong.
o Heart—the soul (mind, emotions, will) or thoughts, feelings, and decisions.
o Become sick—to become weak, tired, wounded, grieved, wore down.

One way to put it is we have many wounded warriors. These wounds are deep, including to the level of personal and national identity. As discussed in chapter 3, loss of identity and cultural integrity creates cycles of disintegration of the family, language, and culture. This level of loss leads to extreme despair, resulting in multiple types of addictions and deviant behaviors.

When people's dreams and desires are dashed over and over again, an inability to dream of better future results. It is safer, less risky, to just settle for the status quo rather than believe God for transformation.

Living in a perpetual state of frustration causes wounds in the soul to be reinforced and amplified with each passing generation. These strongholds set up camp in the recesses of the mind and control thinking, feeling, and acting. Negative patterns of a defeated or cursed mentality create atmospheres that are inviting, conducive, and opportune for dark powers to cultivate evil in the lives of the people.

> We are the generation to break the generation cycles and institute generational blessing!

Just as curses can be passed down from one generation to the next, so can generational blessings. God will always have His remnant on the earth. All the while that hell has been at work, so have living rooms and churches been filled with powerful prayer gatherings to meet and intercede for unsaved loved ones, wayward children, communities, and nations. The prayers of our mothers, grandmothers, and those who have gone before *have not* fallen on deaf ears. Their times of travail and intercession are working, breaking the heavy chains of deeply rooted generational curses. I hear the chains falling!

Warriors Seated in Christ

I am positive that for those of us who are the beneficiaries of such prayer intervention, God did not save us out of the clutches of darkness to sit submissively on the pew of lukewarm religion while hell advances at will. In fact, at the core of every Native American resides the spirit of a *warrior*. If you are still reading this book, I bet you have a bit of a "fighter spirit" in you as well.

Once this warrior spirit is redeemed, (bought back) by the blood of the Lamb, undergone much-needed healing in His glory, sanctified by and surrendered to Jesus, the Captain of the army, and unleashed from a position seated *in* Christ—all I can say is you better look out!

I declare warriors *arise!* Find your post, man and women, your stations! In the last days, the Bible declares: "I will pour out my spirit upon all flesh: and my sons and daughters will rise up and prophesy. Your old men will dream dreams. Your young men will see visions!" (Joel 2:28, KJV) Sons and daughters will rise up and prophesy what they see (dreams and visions) from the spirit world (where God resides).

If His will is to be enforced "On earth, as it is in Heaven," we have to grasp what heaven is saying. "I will stand my watch and set myself on the rampart and watch to see what He will say to me" (Habakkuk 2:1). This is how we gain "vision" for our lives, families, and ministries.

Few things could have motivated me to seek God's pre-ordained plans for NAOMI House, then to come into my role as the leader! It was 2014 when this happened, and my heart cried out on a whole new level to see what God had in mind.

Once we grasp what heaven is saying, by faith, we can establish His will on earth.

I had such an experience not too long ago. I was in prayer one morning for all of my many needs concerning family, ministry, and leading a non-profit, etc. It can get so overwhelming when we are simply conducting the affairs of our life with a natural mindset. This is why the power of spirit-led prayer is paramount.

During this time in prayer, I realized I was ascending towards heaven where I saw in my mind's eye what appeared to be a business meeting in process around a very, very long boardroom table with the Father, Son, and Holy Spirit. The table had people and angels seated all around it. I thought, *"Wow!"* I knew for a fact that this meeting had to do with destiny plans and all those assigned to it. However, I really didn't know what that destiny was or what they were discussing.

I saw a fresh jar of oil beside the One sitting at the head of the table. I came and sat down at the table thinking, *This is so cool.* I wondered, "God, who are all these people?" Suddenly down the runner of this extremely long table, I saw in big, bold, black letters NAOMI House. Inside the letters on the table, I was able to see what appeared to be a "sea of children."

Then I turned, and the One sitting at the head of the table took a deep breath and blew across the whole table. I saw papers flying up in the air. I knew that these papers consisted of heaven's blueprints and His agenda. I saw book manuscripts and organizational structure plans.

As I was contemplating what I was seeing, I heard a voice say, "This breath will cause such a windstorm, a *momentum,* that it will carry with it an entire generation." I then realized that every person around that table was assigned to the many different aspects of God's vision for NAOMI House and to this generation of Native American children.

Intercession can dismantle chaos and enforce Godly order. Colossians 3:1-2 (MSG) makes this challenge:

> So if you're serious about living this new resurrection life with Christ, act like it. Pursue the things over which Christ presides. Don't shuffle along, eyes to the ground, absorbed with the things right in front of you. Look up and be alert to what is going on around Christ—that's where the action is. See things from His perspective.

I'm not saying you have to have a grandiose heavenly vision, hear an audible voice, or similar experience in order to receive instruction from heaven. If you do, that's great! However, most often, it's a simple "knowin' in your knower." We walk by faith and not by sight. It's an everyday relationship and corresponding obedience to the written Word of God that leads us into His plans and purposes.

Reading, hearing, meditating, and studying the Word of God is what will assist us in realizing what heaven is saying about any given situation or need. Faith comes by hearing and hearing by the Word of God (Romans 10:17). Once we *know* that we *know* what God says about it, we can then move forward in faith. The ability to see or divine revelation is what opens up the realm of faith. If you can see it, the corresponding faith to believe it and take it is made available.

If It Matters to You, It Matters to Him

God cares about everything that concerns you today.

I want to share an example of answered prayer, to meet a practical need. Just a few years back, I and my family of four were all living in a 400 square foot efficiency apartment here at NAOMI. We had lived in these staff quarters for over four years. Did you hear me? 400 square feet. To say that it was tiny is an understatement. I didn't even have a normal size refrigerator. No dishwasher. No washer and dryer. You know what? I didn't even have a closet. I'm serious.

One year, NAOMI decided that the summer project for the ministry would be to add an additional 800 square feet to this tiny home. This would make the living space a whopping 1200 square foot, two-bedroom. I mean, this would be like the Taj Mahal for me.

We had set a budget of 75,000 dollars, but mind you, we had 0.00 dollars in the "building fund." As we were getting closer to the time to break ground, one of my Board Members called. "We need money for this addition," he exclaimed! "We need to raise some funds. We need to think of ways that we can bring awareness to this project." I was in my usual element of working and dealing with a myriad of issues that arise daily in a place like ours when he called. Finally, I stopped him. I said, "No! We're going to pray."

Armed with the fact that there is absolutely no financial shortage in heaven, knowing that we are in covenant with almighty God, knowing that God can do anything and without Him, we can do nothing, we went into what I call "ascension prayer." In faith, we rose above the situation, and out of my mouth came: "Lord! We are going to ask You for 50,000 dollars for this project!" I heard the voice on the other end of the line say, "Ummm...Yah! Amen." I said, "Amen."

That summer, we did what we always do, and we began the project by faith. One afternoon that same board member arrived for his annual trip to NAOMI. He was working on the roof one blistering hot afternoon when I got a phone call. "Hello, Genevieve, this is so and so from such and such financial institution. We are requesting your mailing address so that we can send a donation from a private donor." I was busy, busy as usual, so I hurriedly gave her the information. At the last moment, before she hung up, I said, "How much is that donation for?" She said, "Okay, let me look. Oh, yes, it looks like that is a 50,000 dollars donation, ma'am."

You know what? One month later, that same donor sent another check for 25,000 dollars, making a total donation of 75,000 dollars. Our budget was met. To this day, we do not know who that "private donor" was. But I know where it came from! There is *no* shortage or lack in heaven. Do you want to know what else there is no shortage of in Heaven? Stainless steel, full-size refrigerators, dishwashers, washers, and dryers! And also walk-in closets! Praise the Lord.

If God cares about things like walk-in closets, how much more does He have something to say over the nations? How much more does He care meticulously for you today, my brother, my sister?

Destiny Books in Heaven

Psalm 139 speaks of books in heaven that contain original intent. Every person has a personal book. Every kingdom assignment on the earth has a book. Every church, every nation, people group, and region has God-designed intent. These plans have been written in heaven before the foundations of the world. "Your eyes saw my substance, being yet unformed. And in Your book, they were all written, the days fashioned for me, when as yet there were none of them" (Psalm 139:16, NKJV).

The phrase "in thy book" is the Hebrew word *cephar,* which means a register; a legal document or letter of instruction, a written order or decree, a book/scroll of prophecy. A record book in God's index of the living.

The phrase "the days all were written" is the Hebrew word *kathab,* which means all were formed and framed—as a potter with clay—by being squeezed into shape; to destine anything; to form in mind and devise a plan.

Note the phrase "When yet there were none of them." None of what? Days, because they had yet to exist. This is possible because God is outside of the realm of time. Consider the clarity these various versions of Psalm 139:16 bring to the verse:

CEV: "Even before I was born, you had written in your book everything I would do."
TLB: "Every day recorded in your book."
NLT: "Every moment was laid out."
MSG: "The days of my life all prepared before I'd ever lived."

The writings in heaven's books are based on God's original intent. Our journey is to discover what is written in them. Then we must decide if we will partner with Him and enforce what is written so that it is manifest on the earth. God the Father, God the Son (the Word of God), and God the Holy Spirit, our *parakletos,* all stand by eagerly to assist us in the fulfillment of His great plan.

It is awe-inspiring that heaven wants to partner with us on earth. In fact, it's the only way His kingdom can be accomplished. The Kingdom of Darkness is in *the spirit realm* desiring to be released on the earth. The Kingdom of Heaven is in *the spirit realm* desiring to be released on the earth. Either can only be done through people. The spirit realm requires human partnership. When individuals, families, churches, people groups, regions, and nations arise and align themselves with God's plans—it will unlock the Kingdom of Heaven in the earth.

> "Prayer is an earthly invitation for heavenly intervention."
>
> ~Myles Munroe~

Prayer is *how* we partner. Prayer is the portal through which supernatural intervention can occur. Why? Because prayer releases God's power and abilities into our lives and circumstances. Through the power of prayer, we can manifest, demonstrate and release the very presence of God Himself!

Prayer brings guidance and reveals the will of God for a region, a people, or an individual. If we only see from the natural perspective, we will continue to be limited by our temporal circumstances. However, if we will rise above our own limitations and partner with what God is saying and doing, we will begin to see the supernatural take place in our midst.

This is why Colossians 3:1-2 admonishes us to "seek those things which are above, where Christ is, sitting at the right hand of God. Set your mind on things above, not on things on the earth." Verse 3 tells us why: "For you died, and your life is hidden with Christ in God."

Realize God's goodness and promises are not hidden *from* us, they are hidden *for* us. I Corinthians 2:9 reminds us of the incredible *things* which God has prepared for those who love Him, and verse 10 assures us that God will reveal the things to us through His Spirit, which searches the deep things of God. The word *revealed* in verse 10 is the Greek word *apokalypto,* and it is translated: to uncover, lay open what has been veiled or covered up; to disclose, and make bare. To make known or manifest what was before unknown.

When we are tuned in to His voice and His Word, get ready for such revelation. This is exciting, friends. Maybe you are facing a real need today in your life or ministry or family? I want to encourage you to seek out what God says about your situation. If God said it, it's yours, and the devil is a liar! Stand flat-footed in this realm and pull in God's promise from the heavenly realm by faith!

The Spirit of the Lord is on the Move Amongst the First Nations

We are in a unique moment in time in this new era.

"See, I am doing a new thing! Now
it springs up; do you not perceive it? I

am making a way in the wilderness and
streams in the wasteland."
                              Isaiah 43:19 (NIV)

The original host people of American soil have a strategic place and mandate in the Body of Christ. Carrying an
activated warrior spirit and a unique sound that pierces the
spirit realm, could it be possible that the First Nations people
hold the key to unlock revival in America? I think so. If this
is true, and you were the enemy, wouldn't you hit them the
hardest, going to great lengths to "take them out" all together?

When you have experienced such levels of darkness
firsthand, when you have faced seemingly unsurmountable
disparity and evil, there is just something in you that fuels the
passion of Truth and Light! I see the Native American people
from every tribe and tongue rising up as carriers (missionaries) of His presence and power to the rest of America (insert
war-cry here)! Can you hear it? Warriors circle up!

Tipping the Prayer Bowls of Heaven

The Bible talks about the prayers of the saints being
accumulated in bowls in heaven (Revelation 5:8). Think of
a waterpark. There are spots where large buckets hang over-
head filling little by little with water. The closer the bucket
gets to being full, the more anticipation fills the hearts of the
children below. It's coming—*an outpouring is surely coming.*
Then *suddenly,* the bucket tips and a great flood of refresh-
ment crash down on all below!

Revelation 8:3-5 (KJV) reveals:

Then another angel, having a golden censer, came and stood at the altar. He was given onto him much incense, that he should offer it with the prayers of all the saints upon the golden altar which was before the throne. And the smoke of the incense, with the prayers of the saints, ascended before God from the angel's hand. Then the angel took the censer, filled it with fire from the altar, and threw it to the earth. And there were noises, thundering's, lightings and an earthquake.

As the prayers of God's people ascend and accumulate, at some point, just like those water buckets at a water park, the golden bowls with an aroma fill and begin to spill over. At this point, the angel takes the censer, fills it with fire, and releases that "fire from the altar" back down to affect those on earth.

Pastor of Free Chapel, Jentzen Franklin, said this about our prayers,

What a marvelous image! When you pray, you are filling the prayer bowls of heaven. In God's perfect timing, your prayers are mixed with the fire of God (His power) and cast back down to earth to change your situation. Even if you don't feel like anything is happening in the natural world, when you pray, you are filling the prayer bowls in the spirit

> realm. When they are full, they will tilt
> and pour out answers to your prayers.

The power of spirit-led prayer and intercession can shift a nation out of its captivity and break deeply rooted generational strongholds. *The power of collective spirit-led prayer and intercession can break every yoke of bondage over a region and its people,* bringing new life and the ability to dream again. We are right in the middle of such a shift.

The leadership of the Navajo Nation has brought an unprecedented hope and shift over the Tribes of the South West. I'm not saying there has never been a Christian in the Presidential position, but when the President of the Navajo Nation boldly streamed on Facebook his water baptism in the Jordan River in Israel last year, it was evident something was shifting. Talk about tipping the bowls over a Nation!

You could literally see on the video the heavenly activity above our President's head as he went down and came up out of the water. This symbolized a shift. This was an example of fire from the altars sent down from heaven and impacting the events on earth.

This shift has the capacity to impact all of the smaller tribes across America. For example, the enemies' long-standing attempts to establish the diabolical concept that "Jesus is a white man's God" are eroding.

Though He has been so grossly misrepresented in times past, Jesus really is who He says He is—the *one and only* way to Creator. We are in what is called a *kairos* (opportune) moment in time. The prayers of the saints have ascended, filling the bowls that are now tipping.

Concluding Reflections

Native Americans are and have always been spiritual people, praying people, people who love family and community. As America continues to pray to God the Father in the name of Jesus Christ, we will see accelerated answers to our prayers. As non-Natives and Natives unite in healing, humility, partnership, and prayer, such actions will ascend with such a fragrant incense that fire from the altars will return to the earth, bringing a revival in this country like never before seen. As we unite in the power of agreement, we will see people coming to Christ, healings, and deliverances here in America by the masses.

Let us join hands and declare: *"'Thy Kingdom come, Thy will be done, on Earth as it is in Heaven.' Open the books and send the fire of answered prayer, Lord!"*

In fact, let's look at a spiritual super-power that is even stronger than faith. A force that simply cannot be stopped. I am talking about the agape love of God.

12

The Apostolic Anointing

━━━━━━━━⟩)•(⟨━━━━━━━━

"He who sent me is with me.
The Father has not left Me alone,
for I always do those things that please Him."

~John 8:29 (NKJV)~

A Christian missionary is a disciple who is sent into an unfamiliar area to 1) perform ministries of service or to help meet the practical needs of a (usually) different culture or people group, 2) to advocate or promote the kingdom of God and spread the Gospel of Jesus Christ, and 3) at the most basic level, a missionary is someone who has been *sent with a purpose.*

The word "missionary," with its root found in "mission," may not appear in your English Bibles, but it is still a biblical concept. Eckhard Schnabel, one of the world's leading experts on "Missions in the New Testament," makes this point. The Latin verb *mittere* corresponds to the Greek verb *apostellein,* which occurs 136 times in the New Testament (ninety-seven times in the Gospels, used both for Jesus having been "sent" by God and for the Twelve being "sent" by Jesus).

The apostles, in the broadest sense of the term, were those who had been sent out with a purpose. It is the first thing Jesus notes about his mission—he was *sent to proclaim a message* of good news to the poor (Luke 4:18). Being "on mission" or engaging in missions suggests intentionality and advancement.

> Every Christian—if we are going to be obedient to the Great Commission— *must be involved in missions, but not every Christian is a missionary.*

When most people think of mission work, they automatically think of international or Third-World countries. But here in the US, right in our backyard, a mission field exists.

A Sent One: Anointed Carriers of His Presence and Power

You and I are created to be carriers of God's presence, power, purpose, and glory to this generation. Will you respond? In Christ, we are all carriers of the splendors of heaven. Wherever we go, we carry with us His glory, a portable Eden, through the indwelling Holy Spirit.

Second Corinthians 5:20 (AMP) declares that "We are ambassadors for Christ, as though God were making His appeal through us; we [as Christ's representatives] plead with you on behalf of Christ to be reconciled to God." An ambassador in this verse refers to a resident representative of one's own government who is appointed for a special or temporary assignment and given the authority to fulfill the charge. Wherever God sends you, you are on assignment as a representative of Christ. Your charge? To administrate on earth heaven's highest government and highest authority.

A *missionary* who is truly called by God and sent by the Holy Ghost is apostolic. Not necessarily the Office of an Apostle (Ephesians 4:11), but rather the ongoing role of the apostolic—one who carries an apostolic anointing in correlation to an assignment. Sent to a specific place, Christian missionaries carry authority and purpose of setting in heavenly order that which is in chaos. The empowerment of the Holy Spirit upon a Sent One's life has the authority and ability to break spiritual barriers and impart principles and patterns of heaven in an assigned location.

And honestly, you are going to need it! Rest assured, God will not expect you to go out on your own. He *has* equipped His co-laborers with His power and ability!

Every believer is sent into their families and communities, marketplaces, businesses, and areas of influence as representatives and ambassadors for Christ. We are in desperate need of fresh oil and the power of the Holy Spirit upon our lives to impart heavenly order. "So, Jesus said to them again, 'Peace to you as the Father has sent Me, I also *send you.*' And when He had said this, He breathed on them, and said to them, 'Receive the Holy Spirit'" (John 20:21-22).

The Apostolic Anointing is a Breaker Anointing

The Old Testament prophet Samuel filled his horn with holy fragrant oil and set out to Jesse's house in search of the next King. He could not recognize who he was to anoint by his appearance because God looks at the heart. But Samuel was able to identify the future king "by the Spirit."

Samuel's spirit recognized the spirit in David. His kingly-looking brothers passed before Samuel, and all Samuel knew was "Not him." Finally, when they called in the runt who had been tending sheep in the fields, Samuel heard the Lord say, *"Arise, anoint this one."* Samuel took his horn of oil and poured it upon David. The Bible says, "The Spirit of the Lord came upon David from that day forward" (1 Samuel 16:13, NKJV).

This calling on David's life, paired with his obedience, acceptance, and response to his call, created *a set-apart life* smeared with supernatural power and ability to become Israel's first King. 2 Samuel speaks of the "breaker anointing" that was upon David.

> David attacked the Philistines and
> defeated them. Then he said, "I watched
> the LORD break through my enemies like
> a mighty flood." So he named the place
> "The Lord Broke Through."
>
> 2 Samuel 5:20 (CEV)

The anointing on the apostolic is for a breakthrough. Breakthroughs could be defined and summarized as:

➢ To break out, to open up, to break into, to use violence.

➢ The breaker is Jesus Christ, who has broken through all spiritual opposition and gone before us.

➢ Apostolic believers exercise spiritual authority to obtain breakthroughs.

> Apostolic believers are not passive or conservative. They forcefully advance the kingdom of God.

> Apostolic missionaries are called to address the opposition in the territories where they are sent.

> They are mantled with an aggressive anointing to regain the territories and dispose of the current tenants who have taken up residency, possibly for generations.

This anointing omits a fragrance that will apply continual pressure on the kingdom of darkness and establish an atmosphere of heaven. I love the way apostolic and prophetic revolutionist Ryan Lestrange sums it up for us:

> As kingdom people, we are not called to go into a region and adapt to the climate. This is one of the real challenges that apostolic forerunners often face, experiencing pressure to conform to the climate and the culture that we are called to challenge. We must pray radical prayers and stir ourselves up in order to resist the pressure. If we adapt to that which we are called to transform, we will end up bitter and dry. Our oil then will diminish because we have abandoned the pathway that we were set on by God. Apostolic leaders are change agents— mantled with reform. We are called to "shake things up"—birth, govern and

lead. We are never called to sit, settle or be stagnant.

Flowing in the Fragrant Anointing of the Holy Spirit

We must posture ourselves to live in such a way as to flow *with* the power of God and not against His Spirit. Paul warns, "grieve not the Holy Spirit of God" (Ephesians 4:30, KJV). "Grieve" here means to cause sorrow or to resist. The last thing we would want to do is grieve or resist our help!

What does it mean to be anointed or empowered by the Holy Spirit for service? To be anointed by the Lord is to 1) be set aside for the Lord's service, and purpose (consecrated, sanctified, dedicated), and 2) to then be smeared or rubbed down with His power, might, and ability to accomplish that purpose.

It's one thing to know that we are called and have an assignment to fulfill, but it is something else entirely to actually walk it out to completion. The anointing upon our lives is the supernatural empowerment to do what we could *never* do on our own. It is easy to start a thing but much more difficult to finish it or finish it strong. We need the power, might, and ability of Gods' Spirit to rest upon our lives in order to do so.

The anointing oil is a fresh flow of power from heaven upon and through a vessel. Isaiah 61:1 (NKJV) talks about Jesus' anointed purpose. "The Spirit of the Lord is upon Me, because the Lord has *anointed* Me to *preach good tidings to the poor; He has sent Me to heal the brokenhearted, to proclaim liberty to the captives, and the opening of the prison to those who are bound.*" The anointing upon Jesus empowered him to—*fulfill a specific purpose*. Ultimately, that purpose is found in 61:3b (NKJV): "That He may be *glorified*." In all of our anointed pursuits, our ultimate and highest purpose is to bring Glory back to God.

The first chapter of John finds John baptizing Jesus in a river. "I saw the Spirit descending from heaven like a dove, and He *remained* upon Him" (John 1:32, NKJV). Remained here is the Greek word [*me'no*], meaning not to depart; to continue to be present. Like Jesus, when we learn how to work in harmony with our Helper, He will descend upon our lives and remain. Because Jesus walked in a lifestyle pleasing to God, Jesus was never on His own.

Jesus said: "Walk with Me, and work with Me—watch how I do it. Learn the unforced rhythms of grace" (Matthew 11:29, MSG). Knowing that the Spirit of God is present with us, holding our hand and guiding us step by step, is a powerful and comforting truth.

Jesus did not grieve or resist the help of the Holy Spirit. He lived and walked in such a way that was conducive to the presence of the Holy Spirit to remain upon Him. Therefore, He had all power and ability to fulfill Isaiah 61!

The Holy Anointing Oil

The Old Testament talks about a holy oil that Moses used to anoint the Tabernacle and everything in it. Again, to *anoint* means to smear on or rub down in order to consecrate or set apart something for a specific service. The ingredients Moses used represent certain quality "spices" that, when activated upon our lives, will set us apart, allowing the power of the Holy Spirit to remain and operate through us. These quality spices are found in Exodus 30:22-25:

Also take for yourself quality spices—five hundred *shekels* of liquid myrrh, half as much sweet-smelling cinnamon (two hundred and fifty *shekels*), two hundred and fifty *shekels* of sweet-smelling cane, five hundred *shekels* of cassia, according to the shekel of the sanctuary, and a hin of olive oil. And you shall make from these a holy anointing oil, an ointment compounded according to the art of the perfumer. It shall be a holy anointing oil.

To be prepared, consecrated, or set apart for service to the Lord is not something we hear much about anymore. However, the call to frontlines ministry is a fully dedicated service. It will require a *life* under the influence of the supernatural power of the Holy Spirit. We are no match for the powers of darkness or the obstacles we will encounter along the way, but there are supernatural power and provision available.

Quality Spices

I am providing a study in this Chapter regarding these five "quality" spices and what they represent. I encourage you to take some time to study these ingredients Moses used to make this Holy Anointing Oil, as it creates a certain fragrance.

This aroma is what identifies us in the spirit realm, making us dangerous contenders against our enemy and simply irresistible towards heaven.

Myrrh: Purification and Healing

When we live a laid-down life of loyal love to the Lord, the aroma of His presence will permeate our lives and heal our wounds.

Christ the King was offered a mixture of myrrh on the cross (Matthew 27:34, AMP). This spice represents a *death of our own will* and a purification of our desires, decisions, and passions. The life that exemplifies "not my will but yours" and "I am crucified with Christ" omits an aroma.

The process of purification and healing can be a painful one, but it is worth it. The phrase in Psalm 66, "*He laid affliction on our backs,*" means to ordain or appoint. God is not the source of our problems, but He allows certain situations or circumstances in our lives in order to accomplish His bigger plan. As Paul says in Romans 8:28, "We know that *all things* work together for good [for our benefit and His glory], to those who love God, to those who are the called according to His purpose."

"Work together" means to wrought or hammer into shape! Ouch! Sound uncomfortable? God is much more interested in His plans for our lives coming to fruition than in our comfortability. Remember in the midst of the "hammering," there is most definitely a purpose for the pain. Trust the process. Trust the Potter! He is squeezing and molding our lives into a beautiful piece of art.

The Master Perfumer is using all of the pieces of our lives, good and bad, to season, perfume, and anoint our lives.

Calamus: Kingdom Wealth or Finances

In the Old Testament *calamus* represented those who walked in financial integrity; upright, moral, and ethical.

Money is not the root of all kinds of evil, but the *love* of money is (1 Timothy 6:10). Greediness has caused many to stray away from the faith. Mark 4:19 warns us about the deceitfulness of riches having the power to choke out the word and its fruitfulness in our lives.

Money in and of itself is neutral. However, kingdom finances and Godly financial blessing are both necessary and biblical. Mixing *calamus* gave the children of Israel access to wealth, the commanded blessing of the kingdom of heaven. Whoever could garner this spice was considered wealthy and highly blessed.

Trusting God with our finances, returning a tenth to God from the top of our increase, with a joyful attitude, can cause us to tap into a measure of God's provision like nothing else can. Remember, you cannot outgive God. Reward awaits the righteous. Therefore, "let us *not* grow weary while doing good, for in due season we *shall* reap if we do not lose heart" (Galatians 6:9, NKJV).

Cassia: A Life of Prayer and Humility

Cassia represents the aroma your prayer life omits. It is a Hebrew picture of the head bowed down, surrendering to the presence of the King, surrendered, prostrate in prayer.

Cassia is a very fragrant ingredient in the holy oil and has a lot to do with prayers ascending to the heavens into the nostrils of God. Revelation 5:8 speaks of the golden bowls full of incense, which are the prayers of the saints. This spice is symbolic of Israel being His first love—the aroma of the groom. As they walked from nation to nation, they were like a strong fragrance amongst the heathen.

The kingdom is a counterculture. In this world, you are taught to pursue promotions and advancement. But in God's kingdom, it is only when you have learned the aroma of lowering self that true promotion can come. It is a decision. It is not something that happens by accident, but it is intentional.

Not a cheapening of your value in Christ, but rather a lowering of one's opinion of self. Pride is counter-productive in the kingdom. It will stop the flow of power, causing us to walk in disempowerment. The higher you desire to rank in the Spirit, the lower you must go in the natural.

A life of prayer is the fragrance of time spent in God's presence. "Watch and pray lest you enter not into temptation. The Spirit is willing, but the flesh is weak" (Mark 14:38, NKJV). This is the price of *cassia*—time and humility.

Cinnamon: True Worship

Next is the spice and aroma of *cinnamon* on a believer's life, which represents *the fiery passion* that results in true worship. Cinnamon is the spice that represents the aroma emitted from a life that, while under the greatest of pressures or affliction, releases the fragrant anointing of true worship.

Truth be told, most people don't learn to worship right until they have undergone some fiery trials. "Many are the afflictions of the righteous, but the Lord delivers us out them all" (Psalm 34:19, NKJV). Life is hard, full of tests, trials, and obstacles. I love the comfort Psalm 23:4-5 (NKJV) offers:

> Yea, though I walk through the valley of the shadow of death, I will fear no evil; for you are with me; your rod and your staff, they comfort me. You prepare

a table before me in the presence of my
enemies; you *anoint my head with fresh
oil;* my cup runs over.

Cinnamon is sweet. It is both a fragrance and a spice; it
is a rich, full-bodied aroma that permeates the atmosphere
and carries the breakthrough of heaven. This spice represents
someone who serves God with passion and lives life with zeal
for God, residing in the fiery presence of their First Love
(Revelation 2:1). This is one who carries an aroma that stirs
up the fire so as to continue under the greatest of pressures.
These are sons and daughters of God who, no matter what
happens, regardless of the problems or size of the mountain,
are on fire, burning with passion for God. These are the zeal-
ous ones who will lift their hands up in praise and worship,
even in the midst of the wind and the waves.

The fragrance of *cinnamon* is upon the life of a believer
who perceives Psalm 121, "I will look to the hills from whence
comes my help? My help comes from the Lord, who made
heaven and earth." It is not a lazy faith or a floating along
the walk with God. Revelation 3 talks about a church underneath the spell of a lukewarm spirit, neither hot nor cold.
This condition not only hinders the flow of God's power, but
the Bible says the lukewarm are rejected or projected, like
vomit, out of the mouth of God.

The spice of true fiery worship is not developed overnight. This is the believer who has been through some battles,
carries some scars, has weathered the storms of life, and come
to the same conclusion as Paul did in Romans 8:18 (TPT):
"I am convinced that any suffering we endure is less than
nothing compared to the magnitude of glory that is about
to be unveiled within us." God is looking for the fire-starters
who have allowed their hardships to refine them as pure gold.

Hin of Olive Oil: The Holy Spirit

Our final ingredient is a *hin of olive oil*. In Scripture, oil always represents the anointing of the Holy Spirit.

Our decision to surrender our lives under the leading of the Spirit of God is the base property in the anointing oil concoction. Without it, there is no mixture, no aroma. Olive oil is extracted from an olive seed by a rigorous process, including being first crushed, then pressed, refined, and filtered. Your life, your marriage, and family, your ministry is omitting an aroma.

Remember when the Holy Spirit led Jesus into the wilderness for forty days? When Jesus concluded that season of temptation, the Bible says He returned in the *power* of the Spirit (Luke 4:14), and His formal ministry *began*.

When we embark on our wilderness journey and learn how to work *with* the Holy Spirit, it causes the supernatural power of His presence to remain upon our lives and ministries step by step. It causes us to be detected in the spirit world and carry an atmosphere of heaven everywhere we go. The anointing removes our burdens and destroys our yokes inwardly and then empowers us to *break through*.

It is an aromatic and fragrant oil. When Jesus went into a city, the demons cried out in torment, saying: "What have we to do with You, Jesus, You Son of God? Have You come here to torment us before the time?" (Matthew 8:29, KJV) The unclean spirit discerned Jesus approaching their territory, coming closer and closer. The presence of the anointing torments the devil and demons. We are supposed to be the ones doing the tormenting and dispossessing the powers of darkness at work all around us.

Concluding Thoughts

Remember, the mixture that created a sweet-smelling holy anointing oil was compounded (mixed and blended) *according to the art* of the Perfumer with infinite wisdom, intentionality, skill, and expertise.

Regardless of the trial you are now facing, He knows what He's doing. *Never stop. Never give up.* He is accomplishing a glorious end.

Every believer is being called upon to enforce Christ's Victory, empowered by the Holy Spirit.

13

The Agape (Love) of God

←————————— ➤)●(← —————————→

"'And you shall love [agape] the LORD
your God with all your heart,
with all your soul, with all your mind,
and with all your strength.'
This is the first commandment. And
the second, like it, is this:
'You shall love [agape] your neighbor as yourself.'
There is no other commandment greater than these.'"

~Mark 12:30-31 (NKJV)~

Many of us understand and accept the fact that faith is a mighty force. In fact, I've heard it said, and I agree, that faith is the currency of heaven. But I want to point out that 1 Corinthians 13:13 mentions an even more powerful force than faith: "And now abide faith, hope and love, these three; but the greatest of these is *love*."

Galatians 5:6 makes it clear that faith is activated, expressed, and works by *love*. Love is the very foundation by which the power of faith is able to operate.

Agape is the Highest Form of Spiritual Warfare

I want to encourage you not to glaze over this chapter. There are some profound truths here that I believe will bring a fresh exhortation to you. Maybe you see the word "love" or "agape" and think, "Oh yah, I know, I know." What if someone told you they had the key to the highest form of spiritual warfare available to the believer? Would you want to know what it was? Would you want to learn how to become skillful in it? I challenge you to read on.

First Corinthians 13:1-3 makes these comments related to love:

> "Though I speak with the tongues of men and of angels *but have not love,* I have become sounding brass or a clanging cymbal."

The Amplified Version says, "I have become just an annoying distraction."

> And though I have the gift of prophecy, and understand all mysteries and all knowledge; and though I have all faith, so that I could remove mountains, *but have not love,* I am nothing. And though I bestow all my goods to feed the poor, and though I give my body to be burned, *but have not love*, it profits me nothing.

> 1 Corinthians 13:1-3 (NKJV)

Three times in this passage, the phrase "but have not love" occurs. Paul's point was focused on "super-spiritual" people who demonstrate no love. The phrase "sounding brass" means a noise that reverberates or echoes, having a hollow, empty sound when beaten. The phrase "tinkling cymbal" means to clash or to crash constantly and loudly together. The picture Paul paints is that of obnoxious, noisy clashing of metal that produces a hollow, annoying, irritating sound that seems to eternally reverberate.

The word "love" here is the Greek word *agape.* Not all loves are equal. No, definitely not. Agape is in a class all by itself. It is the God-kind of love.

You may have heard it said, "mankind has a God-shaped hole in their soul that only He can fill?" Well, this "love" is what is missing in each one of us. Agape love is a force so deep, so pure, so powerful, so overwhelming that it can literally transform the recipient, never to be the same again. It is God-love. God-breathed, God-inspired, God-shaped. It is agape.

Until we become its beneficiary, we are helpless and hopeless to extend love towards others. But once you've encountered its glorious impact, you can become a portable love bank whereby God's love can be dispersed to a desperate world all around us. However, the reverse is true as well, we cannot give what we do not have.

Dwelling in the presence of God (who is love) puts us on the path to deep spiritual development and transformation that will be seen and felt by others. When this is the primary goal of the believer, he/she is *not* an average Christian but a *dangerous* Christian.

Here are a few definitions and descriptions of the power of agape (love):

o   Agape demonstrates God's immeasurable and incomparable love for humankind.
o   Agape is an ongoing, outgoing, self-sacrificing concern for others.
o   God gives this agape love without condition and unreservedly to those who are undeserving and inferior to Himself.
o   God does not *have* agape love. God *is* agape love (1 John 4:16).
o   We love Him because He first loved us (1 John 4:19).
o   Agape love gives. "For God so loved the world that He gave" (John 3:16).
o   We have been brought near to God (agape love) by the blood of Jesus (Ephesians 2:12-13).
o   Agape is an intentional, self-sacrificial love inspired by God's love *for* us, operating *through* us.

Disciples of Love are Recognized in the Spirit

Truly, the most powerful spiritual weapon that God has given us is His love, even trumping the super-power of faith.

Right after His resurrection and before His ascension, Jesus gave final instructions to His disciples: "go therefore and make disciples" (Matthew 28:18-19). John 13:34-35 lets us know how to recognize a disciple:

> "A new commandment I give to you, that you love one another; as I have loved you, that you also love one another.
> *By this* all will know that you are my disciples, *if you have love [agape]* for one another."

There is a distinct characteristic of a true disciple of Christ, and that is love. The Great Commission declaring "go therefore and make disciples" could be read, "go therefore and teach my people how to agape."

John 13:25 (MSG) says, "This is how everyone will recognize my disciples. When they *see* the love you have for each other." When agape is demonstrated to a lost and dying world by God's people, then all will recognize that we are disciples of Christ.

However, it's not only those in the physical realm that recognize demonstrated love. The spirit world will also recognize it and be forced to take notice of a believer who walks in this super-power.

I have read the story of the Seven Sons of Sceva in Acts 19:11-17 (NKJV) many times, but recently the Lord showed me an interesting perspective that connects the power of agape to the spirit world. I'll quote it here:

> Now God worked unusual miracles by the hands of Paul, so that even handkerchiefs or aprons were brought from his body to the sick, and the diseases left them, and the evil spirits went out of

them. Then some of the itinerant Jewish
exorcists, took it upon themselves to call
the name of the Lord Jesus over those
who had evil spirits, saying, 'we exorcise
you by the Jesus who Paul preaches. And
the evil spirit answered and said, "Jesus I
know, and Paul I *know*, but who are you?
Then the man in whom the evil spirit was
leaped on them, *overpowered* them, and
prevailed against them, so that they fled
out of that house naked and wounded.
This became known both to all Jews and
Greeks dwelling in Ephesus; and fear fell
on them all, and the name of the Lord
Jesus was magnified.

The demon spirits' comments concerning Paul in verse
15 is what really stuck out to me: "And the evil spirit answered
and said, 'Jesus I *know*, and Paul I *know*, but who are you?'"
Check out a couple of these Bible translations of this verse:

- Amplified Bible: "I know about Paul…"
- Christian Standard Bible: "I recognize Paul…"
- Common English Bible: "I am familiar with
  Paul…"
- The Message Version: "I have heard about Paul…"

We can easily see why these demons recognized Jesus,
I mean, He is Jesus. But it made me ask, why did the spirit
world recognize Paul? How did they hear about him? What
kind of conversations would they have had about Paul, his
apostleship and spiritual authority?

There very well may be a long list of answers to this question, but I thought it so interesting that it was Paul who wrote 1 Corinthians 13—the "agape chapter." He, inspired by the Holy Spirit, penned the fifteen-bullet point list of the definition of love (which I provide in the next pages), which ends by saying: "And now abide faith, hope and love, these three; but the greatest of these is love."

The word "greatest" means larger, stronger in space and dimension (measurement and height). There is a dimension in agape love. A realm that creates a measurable capacity to house virtue, authority, and power. It is a larger and more expansive container than the vessel of great faith or great hope (expectation). The greatest of these is *love*.

It was Paul who also wrote 2 Timothy 1:7: "God has not given us a spirit of fear, but of power, *love* (agape) and of a sound mind." You see, Paul knew a thing or two about the power of agape. As a result, hell had to recognize and defer to his authority when he showed up!

According to 1 John 4:18: "There is no fear in love; but perfect love *casts out* fear because fear involves torment [to vex, harass, and distress]." To cast out means to drive it out, throw it out, or to expel. Fear is just one example of a demonic spirit, and love "casts it out." Demons cried out in torment and fear when Jesus even came into their vicinity (Matthew 8:29). Why? Because Jesus was the living, breathing, walking, talking expression of pure love.

As for us, we cannot give what we don't have. We are to be *made perfect* in love (1 John 4:18b). This is not speaking of our perfection, no. We (you and I) are to grow or mature in the revelation of God's love. It's a conviction that grows daily—He really loves me; I am perfectly loved by Him, and this truth is driving back and casting out fear.

The Greatest Commandment

Apart from the power of God, we are no match for our enemy. If we attempt to fight in the flesh, we will lose each and every time. First Corinthians 9:26 offers this challenge: "I therefore run [strike hard and exert all effort in order to overcome], not as uncertainly [without definite and clear aim; so fight I not as one that beats the air [striking repeatedly and forcefully in vein; having no effect]." The NLT translates it this way: "So I run with purpose in every step. I am not just shadowboxing."

Fighting in the flesh is like running on a treadmill— exerting a lot of energy, making a lot of noise, but wasting a lot of time. Fighting darkness with darkness never wins. Attempting to fight with weapons like anger, jealousy, unforgiveness, manipulation, confusion, or depression won't work.

Mark 12:30-31 (NKJV) reads:

> "And you shall love the Lord your God with all your heart, with all your soul, with all your mind, and with all your strength. This is the first *commandment.* And the second, like it, is this: you shall love your neighbor as yourself. There is no other commandment *greater* than these."

Interestingly, the word "commandment" in this verse is the Greek word *"entole,"* which literally means *prescription.* The word "greater" is the Greek word *"meizon,"* which means stronger or strongest. The agape (love) of God is the strongest prescription known to the human race. When we receive God's love for us, there is nothing that love cannot heal, cure, or break through. There is no wrong that agape cannot make right. When we operate in the agape of God towards others, it works as an antidote to everything opposing the kingdom of God. It has the power to overthrow the hardest of hearts and replace them with a soft heart; it makes souls whole.

Receiving and growing in God's love does not happen overnight. That is especially true for many of us who have experienced trauma, abuse, or a poor example of love by our earthly fathers. I remember hearing testimony by Joyce Meyer. She went through horrible sexual abuse throughout the entirety of her childhood. Her testimony includes that she had to study the subject of God's love in His Word for a solid year before she could even begin to grasp and accept this truth. She now has a worldwide ministry. Through powerful preaching and teaching of God's Word, she now sees many captives set free by the power of God's agape.

The Agape of God

Here is a reminder of the characteristics of agape according to 1 Corinthians 13. Normally the only time we would hear this section of Scripture or look at it at all is when recited at the altar of a wedding ceremony.

But don't forget that these characteristics manifested in our lives are how we are recognized as His disciples both in this world and in the spirit world. Growing in these attributes is a command of God that results in carrying atmospheres of freedom and deliverance.

These features include:

1. Longsuffering
2. Kindness

3. Does not Envy
4. Does not parade itself
5. Is not puffed up
6. Does not behave rudely
7. Does not seek its own
8. Is not provoked
9. Thinks no evil
10. Does not rejoice in iniquity
11. Rejoices in the truth
12. Bears all things
13. Believes all things
14. Hopes all things
15. Endures all things

Love never fails (falls to the ground powerless)!

Being Developed in the Love of God

The time we spend soaking in God's Word, in His love, and in His presence will result in maturing sons and daughters. That is because we become a reflection of the One to which we have a relationship. He is kind. He is humble. He is forgiving. He is love. To the degree that we spend time with Him is to the degree of our testimony resulting as this—"the enemy has no claim on me" (John 14:30, AMPC).

Jesus is the One with all authority, power, dominion, and rule. Second Timothy 2:12 (NKJV) testifies: "We shall also reign with Him [if we suffer with Him]." It doesn't always feel good to turn the other cheek. We won't always feel like treating people right who do us wrong. Walking in forgiveness, even with all of Jesus' authority and power at our disposal, is not the easiest pill to swallow.

The pangs and cries of suffering are just the sound of the fleshly spirits before they find their official and final exit from our life. Every single time your flesh cries out in torment when you choose to walk in love, realize you are being set free more and more. When we train ourselves to respond in love rather than in the flesh, when it hurts the most, it is in those very moments that your spirit is taking the driver's seat. When this becomes a lifestyle or way of life, we are granted permission to operate or advance in authority and power in the Spirit. Remember, a true disciple is marked by their love walk.

Maturing in agape and walking according to the Spirit and not the flesh is how we gain spiritual strength. But, understand it is a process that is often a painful one. Unchecked emotions, thoughts, and decisions can hinder us from living in the realm of love. They must be surrendered daily and continually. This process repeats until we have the rule over them. We then are a house no longer divided but a new person in Christ with a single focus.

Truly some of the most powerful tools that a Christian has are the fruit of the Spirit (Galatians 5:22-23). These fruit, or evidence of the Spirit at work in your life, are not wimpy or powerless. These are weapons of mass destruction against your enemy and his tactics. Love is a fruit of the Spirit and the most powerful one at that.

I believe that the spirit world takes notice when we walk in self-sacrificial love, forgiveness, and honoring others in humility. The way we treat people, the way we respond to situations and adverse circumstances are all felt and heard by those around us. But they are also recorded in the unseen realm.

Think about it. You really can't live a life of bitterness and unforgiveness and be powerful at the same time. This is why developing our love walk can be so important! Because love has nothing in common with hatred. Love is the opposite of darkness; it is the opposing force to evil.

As mentioned in a previous chapter, Jesus' testimony in John 14:30 (AMP) was this, as it pertains to the *prince of this world*: "He has no claim in Me. [He has nothing in common with Me; there is nothing in Me that belongs to him, and he has no power over Me]." Jesus walked in all power because everything He did was the opposite of His adversary.

Those who are born again have a spirit man that is spotless, righteous, and made perfect before God (thank You, Jesus)! But it is the soulish realm that can have things in common with darkness.

For example, kindness is the Greek word *chresteuomai,* which means to be adaptable or compliant to the needs of others. This is a super-power and antidote to selfishness. Anyone can be self-centered, mean-spirited, and cold. Genuine agape doesn't think of itself first. Instead, it always reaches out, focusing primarily on the needs of others.

Remember, Acts 19:16 describes how things that belong to the enemy can leap on us, overpower us, and prevail against us when we are not walking as Jesus prescribes. Dealing with wounded, envious, arrogant, jealousy-driven individuals? Do not allow what is on them the legal right to jump on you because you have something in common with it.

Like Jesus, we too can and must "overcome [master over and defeat evil] with good" (Romans 12:21, NKJV).

See Appendix A, which identifies Practical ways to increase your love walk, and Appendix B for an extended study of 1 Corinthians 13.

Binding the Strongman

In Matthew 12:22-30 (NKJV), Jesus put it like this when casting out demons (like those listed above), and the religious rulers accused him of relying on the power of Beelzebub to cast out demons:

> Jesus knowing their thoughts, said to them, "Every kingdom divided against itself is brought to desolation, and every city or house divided against itself will not stand. If Satan casts out Satan, he is divided against himself. How then will his kingdom stand? But if I cast out demons *by the Spirit of God*, surely the kingdom of God has come upon you. Or how can one enter a strong man's house and plunder his goods unless he first binds the strong man? And then he will plunder his house."

How do you walk in the authority of God against demonic forces who harass and torment at every opportunity? How do you bind up the strong man, whether related to a person, a place, a people, a territory, a nation? The answer is by the Spirit of God, who is *love*. Our authority is not by might, nor by power, but by the Spirit of God (love).

Spiritual promotion only comes from God. But it has a prerequisite—humility. Resurrection *power* came *after* the crucifixion. Philippians 2:15-11 (NKJV) is a powerful description of exactly what I am saying,

> Let this mind be in you which was also in Christ Jesus, who, being in the form of God, did not consider it robbery to be equal with God, but made Himself of no reputation, taking the form of a bondservant, and coming in the likeness of men. And being found in appearance as a man, He *humbled Himself and became obedient* to the point of death, even the death on the cross. Therefore, God also has highly exalted Him and has given Him the Name which is above every name, that at the Name of Jesus every knee should bow, of those in heaven, and of those on earth, and of those under the earth, and that every tongue should confess that Jesus Christ is Lord, to the Glory of God the Father.

Whew! Try to tell me love is weak or powerless! My God!

God Demonstrated His Love by Sending His Son Jesus

Jesus demonstrated His love for us in that "while we were yet sinners Christ died for us" (Romans 5:8, NKJV). Jesus' acts of humbleness and obedience to His Father are the reasons why His Name carries weight across the expanse of the universe. His demonstration of love and humility is what gives the resurrection *power*.

The name Jesus or, in Spanish, *Jesús* is just a name until there is the weight of love, humility, and obedience behind it. Again, in Philippians 2:15, Paul writes, "Let this same mind be in *you*." What?! To those who have decided to pick up their cross (surrendered) and follow after Jesus' example, even at the expense of the burning up their flesh, *will arise in resurrection power*. These are the ones who will make demons tremble and torment them with their very presence. Like Jesus and Paul, these are the ones who will be recognized in the spirit world and carry the weight that is behind the precious name of the resurrected Jesus.

God's Justice System

But it's not fair! I get it. The truths described here are not for the faint of heart. Learning to shift our focus and trust in God and His ways is paramount.

Romans 12:17-21 (AMPC) gives us seven practical ways to "*leave the way open*" for God's Justice System:

> Repay no one evil for evil but take thought for what is honest and proper and noble [aiming to be above reproach] in the sight of everyone.
> If possible, as far as it depends on you, live at peace with everyone.
> Beloved, never avenge yourselves [obsessed with taking revenge], *but leave the way open* for God's wrath; for it is

written, vengeance is Mine, I will repay
says the Lord.

But if your enemy is hungry, feed
him; if he is thirsty, give him drink; for
by so doing, you will heap burning coals
upon his head.

Do not let yourself be overcome by evil
but overcome (master) evil with good.

To heap coals of fire on a person's head initially paints a
picture of burning pain, but it really is not. Instead, it seems
to be a picture of stirring up the coals of a fire to rouse it
back to life again. It is a picture of stirring within a person a
response of remorse once they see your *kindness* in the face of
their meanness.

1. Repay no one evil for evil (Verse 17).
2. Aim to live above reproach in the sight of all others through pursuing what is honest, proper, and noble in any given situation (Verse 17).
3. Live peaceably with all men (Verse 18).
4. Avenge not yourself, meaning do not protect or defend yourself. Do not punish a person for a thing (do not be obsessed with taking revenge or retaliate for a wrong suffered) (Verse 19).
5. Win your enemies with kindness (Verse 20).
6. This will result in heaping coals of fire upon his head, meaning; your surprising generosity will awaken his [deadened] conscience [helping him realize his wrong] and give an opportunity for repentance, reconciliation, or whatever the case demands (Verse 20).
7. Overcome every evil with an act of good (Verse 21).

When we relinquish to God our right to take revenge, we *show faith in His justice.* God will bring conviction upon the one in error. Responding the way Jesus did to His enemies allows the "burning coals" of God's righteousness and justice to operate within the soul of that person, providing a pathway to repentance.

Concluding Reflections

Each and every decision we make to choose love will overpower darkness. Every time we intentionally choose love, not when it's comfortable or convenient, but when the circumstance calls for it, we are waging spiritual warfare (1 Timothy 1:8). The courageous Christ-follower who chooses to pick up his/her cross and follow Jesus no matter what the cost is not the *average* Christian, rather a *dangerous* Christian.

Welcome soldier to another level of dominion and authority. Your enemy never wanted you to hear this. But I declare it's too late.

This next section is full of practical information for first responders, including:

➤ Our need for a National Campaign of Awareness for Native American children and the need for Safe Houses for children on our reservations.

➤ Ten Practical Ways YOU Can Become an Educator and an Advocate Today!

➢ Practical tips for those who feel called to the front lines of Native American ministry, from seasoned missionaries.

➢ A collection of scriptures and powerful prayers

PART 3

————————>)•(<————————

Arise and Mobilize

"Arise, shine; For your light has come!
And the glory of the LORD is risen upon you.
For behold, the darkness shall cover the earth,
And deep darkness the people;
But the LORD will arise over you,
and His glory will be seen upon you.
Then Gentiles shall come to your light
And kings to the brightness of your rising."

~Isaiah 60:1-3 (NKJV)~

14

Educate and Advocate

"For I know the thoughts that I think toward you,
says the LORD, thoughts of peace and not of evil,
to give you a future and a hope."

~Jeremiah 29:11 (NKJV)~

One day, after speaking to a social worker who needed a safe place for three siblings, I was feeling particularly frustrated. I expressed to her once again, "We do not have any room!" She understood and hung up the phone.

I am often asked: "Where do the children go when they are unable to be placed at NAOMI?" And honestly, I am *not* 100 percent sure. Some are forced to stay in adverse circumstances, while others may find a bed at another facility or home.

In any event, after we hung up, I cried out to God, "*God! Help!*" I then had an idea that I believed was from Him. Our twenty-five-plus kids were playing basketball outside my kitchen window, so I grabbed three currently placed children who were the average size of a three-sibling group. I had them hold hands and walk away from me into the sunset. I then posted the picture with the caption and comment. "NAOMI needs your help! We just turned away another sibling group of three children due to a lack of space." (see Photo #9 on page 244)

Of course, people are sympathetic, but we have yet to lay out specific and practical ways that people can jump right in and provide tangible assistance. NAOMI House has been in emergency mode basically since its inception. I truly believe that if people had a clear understanding of the issues and a plan of action for their involvement, they would be more than willing to do what they can.

Towards the end of this chapter, I provide a list of *Ten Practical Ways You* (the reader), *Can Become an Educator and Advocate Today.*

> "Let us put our minds together and see what life we can make for our children."
>
> ~Chief Sitting Bull~

Educate! Educate! Educate!

Educating, advocating, and raising awareness concerning life for Native American children, youth and families are ongoing.

Oftentimes when we think of missionary work, we envision a third-world country across the ocean. It is true that we should go wherever the Lord sends us, near or far. But this mission message of hope in Jesus Christ is also needed *right here* in the US.

Statistics Concerning Native American Children, Youth and Families

- **Child Abuse and Neglect**

  A report of child abuse is made every ten seconds.

  At least five children die every day from child abuse (National Clinical Assessment Service).

- **Alcohol Abuse**

  Alcohol abuse in the Native American community is epidemic.

  More tribal youth die from alcohol than from any other drug (The Indian Reporter).

- **Domestic Violence**

  Three-fourths of Native American women have experienced some type of sexual assault (American Indian Women's Chemical Health Project).

- **Child Sexual Abuse**

  One of the most destructive problems affecting children in Indian Country today is sexual abuse (molestation and rape).

- **Other Issues**

  Young Native Americans today live their lives surrounded with and immersed in poverty, hopelessness, and despair and suicide.

Because of the gut-wrenching brokenness, darkness, and injustice, I feel that now is the time to make our voices heard! Safehouses like NAOMI House are greatly needed on or near most reservations in America.

How can people get involved if they are unaware? Many people do not even know NAOMI House exists or why such a need persists. The power of each child's journey also needs to be revealed. Such stories include the realities of not only overwhelming trauma and difficult circumstances but of strength, resilience, and cycle-breaking hope for the future.

Many people want to know the underlying issues. What are the problems? But more importantly, what are the solutions? These are important questions to ask. I pray that this book has helped shed some light on these areas. The following is something I wrote for an informational video to answer these kinds of questions related to trauma and the need for homes like NAOMI:[7]

NAOMI House (NH), located in Northern Arizona, is an emergency shelter contracted by the Navajo Nation. NH serves Native American children in need.

NH's heart desire is to extend our mission into the South Dakota region, the home of the great Sioux Nation, to serve the Lakota families, children and community.

Founded in 1993, NH has had the privilege of extending the love of Jesus Christ to hundreds of God's precious children.

NH's largest-scale dream is that each of these children be reunified with their biological families in a safe and loving environment. Until then, NH and its incredible staff, donors, and countless volunteers serve on the frontlines around the clock.

Beneath the resilience and beauty of childhood lie extreme peril and often unspeakable trauma for far too many. We believe it is important to shed light to the best of our ability on the realities of growing up indigenous in America today.

With so much brokenness, so much darkness, so much pain and hurt for too many Native American children, we believe we have a responsibility to give them a voice. If we don't speak up for them, who will? If we don't give them hope, who will?

Native American children suffer from abuse at one of the most alarming rates in our country. Child sexual abuse in Native America is both epidemic and holocaustic. Ninety percent of the children who come to live at NH are the victims of child molestation and/or rape.

There is an entire generation of mothers and fathers who have been wartorn by generational cycles of bondage, defeat, and trauma.

Children are in constant jeopardy due to alcoholism, domestic violence, and parental incarceration.

Because of the epidemic of a drug called meth, the death and murder rates are inconceivable. We have had multiple children come to us after the murder of their siblings by their own parent's family members or domestic partners.

A place like NH is actually needed on or near most reservations in America. In fact, right now, there is a child in need of a safe place who will have nowhere to go.

A Kingdom Campaign of Awareness

My question is this: *With the power of darkness shouting so loudly, can we afford to remain silent?*

When fully implemented, the mission of our advocating efforts is to give a voice to the voiceless. Raising awareness is the initial step to create the dialogue necessary for the possibility of lasting change.

I sense a real burden to educate people and then equip that individual as an educator and an advocate! Explaining the gravity and oftentimes dark issues that plague Native American children and families on a daily basis is important. *But I don't want to stop there.* At the very same time, I seek to protect, nurture and maintain the integrity and beauty of the culture and the people.

The truth is Native American people possess a very unique and God-given purpose on the earth. All First Nations people possess talents and unique gifts. Natives are some of the most talented, creative, family-centered, and spiritual people you will ever meet. I am honored to serve amongst each one.

Big-Picture Goals for NAOMI House

One of my goals as a visionary, servant of the Lord, and of children is to bring together an army of people from every corner who can put our God-fearing minds together and collectively address these bigger-picture questions. How do we come alongside or undergird the healing of a generation of children and families? I would love for that group to consist of kingdom-minded Native American leaders as well as the non-native community. Unified around a specific effort, along with boots on the ground, intervention and miraculous change *can and will* happen.

I envision a united effort to implement and sustain lasting change through our current vehicle of safe houses. While we have greater hopes for our children than a warm bed, a loving pseudo-family, and meals until the age of eighteen, the reality is, this piece is vitally important in the big picture.

As of now, NAOMI House operates on an emergency basis. That is, providing food, clothing, shelter, safety, and lots of prayers, all at the drop of a hat, as the immediate need arises. Again, this is an extremely important element.

However, at the heart of NAOMI House is *family*. Why? Because that is what is at the heart of Father God. At the end of the day, *these children have families*. While meeting the everyday emergency needs of children, how can we also strive to facilitate healing, wholeness, and reunification of families in a healthy, safe, and loving environment? Truly, success is not building more houses, with more beds, for more children. *Ultimately, success is the healing and wholeness of the family unit.*

Another goal would be to ultimately move from a defensive, emergency stance. We must *also* be able to operate from a proactive and preventative position as well. Such an approach would fill a major gap evident in the larger problem. We must broaden our scope and vision for American Indian children, youth, families, and communities; by addressing such questions as:

o What are the best ways to continue voicing and advocating, locally and nationally, the atrocities that First Nations families face while yet preserving the integrity of the people and the culture?

o How can our safe houses become sustainable and replicable to continue to meet needed emergency services in Arizona, but also in South Dakota and beyond?

o How can we identify and develop each child's spiritual giftings and God-given purpose?

o How do we move beyond our current mission of "Providing a safe and loving home to Native American children in need" to fostering the bigger picture of reunited, healed, and healthy families and hope for our communities?

o What transitional living assistance, programs, vocational and life-skills training can we provide for kids who are "aging-out" after a lifetime in the foster care system?

o Beyond prayer and VBS (Vacation Bible School), how can we address the underlining generational issues of marginalization and the effects of emotional and physical trauma?

Help for Children; Healing for Families; And Hope for our Native American Communities; is an honorable mission, and it will take a village of unified effort to accomplish.

Ten Practical Ways YOU Can Become an Educator and Advocate Today

Maybe you are wondering, "Okay, Genevieve, but what about me?" I'm so glad you asked! Quite possibly, you, the reader, are not called to the front lines of ministry. But you can still help!

I first want to say thank you from the bottom of my heart *for reading this book* and being willing to listen and learn. It might not seem like much, but each person who takes the time to hear the stories and a desire to engage at any level means more than you know. Each one of you who provides an ear to hear *you* are accommodating the healing of the one with the story. Thank you.

Now I want to share with you ten very practical and simple ways you can be an educated advocate today.

- ✓ Recommend *this Book* and/or the link [www.pre-paringforthecall.com] to your family friends, community, church, a missions' pastor, or the next stranger you meet.
- ✓ Recommend *this Video* https://youtu.be/KftCK0-pP-s to your family, friends, community, church, a missions' pastor, or the next stranger you meet.
- ✓ Share the links to your Facebook wall, all social media outlets, and email network.
- ✓ "Like" us on Facebook and share our page! (https://www.facebook.com/NAOMIHouseAZ)

✓ Purchase items on Amazon and have them sent. View our Practical Needs List here: www.thenaomihouse.org/getinvolved.

✓ Send a monitory donation. Click the link to make a one-time or monthly donation. www.thenaomihouse.org/getinvolved.

✓ OR, mail a check to: NAOMI House—PO Box 205, Joseph City, Arizona 86032

✓ Subscribe! Become a member of the NAOMI House Tribe at www.thenaomihouse.org/getinvolved for regular updates.

✓ Become a prayer partner! www.thenaomihouse.org. Commit to praying for our children and staff through our Prayer Patron Program.

✓ Host a "Campaign of Awareness" gathering. This can be in your Living Room or Invite us to your church or mission's event. www.thenaomihouse.org/getinvolved.

✓ Assemble a work-group of volunteers to spend a day or three or a week on the mission field. www.thenaomihouse.org/getinvolved.

Concluding Reflections

Now is the time to begin, or continue, discussions concerning Native American children and their present needs. With urgency, let us create a space at the table for our First Nations brothers and sisters who hold an intracule place in the Body of Christ. Unlocking God's restorative work amongst our vulnerable in this country hinges upon the power of God's love flowing through all of God's people.

While shedding much light on the immediate needs and hardships of Native American children, my desire is to also acknowledge and declare the spiritual awakening and movement that is currently taking place amongst the Tribes of America.

Salvation through Jesus Christ is sweeping through the First Nations lands. Holding their key of authority as the original inhabitants of the land, explosive kingdom advancement is upon us. Native Tribes are moving full force into their God-given purpose, destiny, and assignment over the nation.

Sowing into the lives of Native children is paramount in this hour. We will soon see a shift from the need to extend a "helping hand" in this generation to hanging onto the coattails of the Native-Christian leadership of tomorrow as whole families become reconciled.

We are a resilient people! It is not over, and the best is yet to come. Merriam-Webster Dictionary defines "resilience" as the capacity to recover quickly from difficulties, the ability to spring back. Resilience means knowing how to cope in spite of setbacks, barriers, or limited resources. Resilience is a measure of how much you want something and how much you are *willing* to overcome every obstacle in order to get it.

Now, for those who *are* called into full-time ministry. In the next chapter, I want to provide some very practical tips to prepare yourself.

15

Practical Tips for First Responders

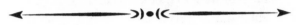

> The Lord said to Abram, 'Leave your land, your family,
> and your father's household for the
> land that I will show you.'

~Genesis 12:1 (CEB)~

This chapter provides practical insights for those called to Native American missions based on a survey conducted with frontline workers. For non-natives in particular, to be called to Native American Ministry means to be called to people with a different history, culture, and language, and therefore a very different perspective of life and worldview. Having a heart's desire to become a student, a learner, is central to the effectiveness of this endeavor.

There is a God-given purpose for all First Nations people. Your job is to tap into what He is already doing and simply facilitate the bigger picture. We do this by meeting the practical and specific daily needs of those in front of us. In this case, the demanding, real-time needs of children who have been deeply wounded and often left with invisible scars.

Whether you are an intern, a family, a volunteer group, a board member, a mission's pastor, or a church group, a deep heart-posture of prayer is required. Prayer reflections along these lines, for example:

> Lord, show me how to serve a different culture and nation that has its own specific beauty and potential, as well as specific issues, injustices, and hardships. Help me to remain humble, always teachable, and prayerful as I step into my new assignment to facilitate the expansion of Your kingdom. I am here to learn and to serve Your name, Jesus. Amen.

The following survey was conducted several months ago with a handful of non-Native missionaries with five or more years of experience serving among Native Americans. A question-and-answer format was used to ascertain practical tips and helpful information for those heading into Native American ministries. Each of the ten survey questions asked is followed by the answers of the various participants in their own words.

Survey Questions and Responses

1. *What do you wish you would have known about working with Native American children on the mission field before stepping into it?*

"The depth of spiritual darkness, and magnitude of the spiritual battle that is going on over reservations and young people."

➢ Finding and securing a prayer covering from believers you know and trust who will truly pray and ask you for prayer requests regularly is very important.

➢ Having a personal, developed "quiet time" with God is vital. You cannot do this type of work on your own strength. At all!

"The workload is fluctuating and also, never-ending."

➢ I was used to working a nine-to-five position, having weekends off. That is usually not the case on the ground.

➢ The magnitude of not only the emotional pain but also of the spiritual struggle of children that seems to persist twenty-four hours a day, seven days a week, is shocking! I wish I would have known more about the effects of trauma on the human soul.

➢ Also, "Indian time" is real! There is no hurry. This goes for doctor visits, social services, etc. Get over it! You are on their time, and no matter how much you want to speed up the process, it is out of your control.

"The Jesus Complex is real."

➢ You are not the savior! It is common to think before coming into a position like this that you are going to be the superhero in this story. The truth is, *only Jesus* is the answer. You are simply the vessel that He will use to get that accomplished. You are not the *answer* to the problem but rather the *messenger* of the problem solver.

"Those you are called to serve are not automatically going to like you."

➤ In some ways, you represent the reason why they are not able to be with their family. No matter how kind you are or how capable you may be, it can feel like you are a punching bag, metaphorically speaking, of course.

"Your time is not your own"

➤ Yes, you may establish a routine, but just *be ready* for *your schedule* to be rudely interrupted. This includes your sleep schedule, your me-time schedule, your errands schedule, whatever the case may be.

"You are going to be tested in *every* way possible. Period."

➤ Your patience will run thin. Your marriage will be tested. Your character will be tested, and you may feel at times that you have made a big mistake by coming onto the mission field.

➤ You are going to see the good, bad, and ugly within yourself, your spouse, and others. Understand that this is a refining process. Realize the refining process is intense. It is made to make or break.

"I had no idea what I was about to encounter."

> God's call on my life to minister to Native American children was, without a doubt, one of the most powerful callings I had ever had. I was elated to move to Arizona and knew the Lord was sending me to work with these very precious children. However, I had no idea what I was about to encounter.

"I wish I had learned about real Native American history in school or heard about it in the news."

> I was broken-hearted to learn how terrible Native Americans had been abused by our government and even more so by early missionaries—all in the Name of Jesus.

"I wish I had known more about Native Americans and reservation life."

> The needs are deeper than *poverty*. Hundreds of years of neglect and persecution from the American government have created great anguish, harm, and damage.

> Many of the first white missionaries sinned against our Native people so badly that Christianity is looked down upon by many Native Americans and considered to be 'the white man's religion.'

"I wish I had been able to live on a reservation beforehand and had actually experienced the pain and difficulties only found by living with our First Americans."

> The needs are tremendous. I had absolutely no idea of the depth of trauma and woundedness.

2. *What are some of the things you have learned about yourself since experiencing mission work?*

"I have come to realize that I was too proud."
> I am selfish, I have had an easy, or should I say, "privileged" life. Friendships used to come easily. They don't anymore. I am more joyful and peaceful than I have ever been."

> I have come to learn that I am capable of handling a lot more than I ever thought I could. I realize now that I am not in control of my own life. God is in control. The more I stop fighting Him, the more blessings I see. I've learned the heart of God. He sees these children and knows them inside and out. He wants them to know His love, and I have learned that I am in a position of surrendering to Him (like a bridge) so that he can get to these kids through me.

> What have I learned? Well, it's not about me. It's all about Jesus. Without Christ, I am nothing. The children need Jesus, not me. My gifts, my talents are nothing without Christ's anointing.

3. *How has being a missionary affected your personal family? In what ways? Positively and/or negatively?*

    ➤ Here, there is persecution of Christians, so you are less likely to be lukewarm. For that, I am grateful.

    ➤ It has been a challenge learning how to adjust to the challenges of parenting more than just your biological children in a group setting. However, my kids have learned the influence they have here is so important. They have learned compassion and patience.

    ➤ Because of the fact that wounded people hurt other people, some of my children were hurt by the children I was ministering to. They were also blessed in many ways, enjoyed many happy times, and made lifelong friends they still keep in touch with. Some of my children are now ministering to abused children.

4. *How has being a missionary affected your personal world views, mindsets, perspectives, or beliefs?*

    ➤ It has made me keenly aware of my attitudes toward minorities—my preconceived ideas from childhood. It has affected my attitude toward the poor. They don't need what I have. They are strong. They need to learn that Jesus loves them and died to be in a relationship with them. People in poverty don't need junk. They need respect and challenges to become who they were created to be.

> The mission field is an entirely different world. It can be comparable to someone who has been to the battlefield during the war. They have a completely different perspective. Their focus is not church picnics or game night. They are too busy fighting for their lives and the lives of others. That is my perspective of what I do.

> Visiting large, prosperous churches sometimes grieves me now. I didn't realize that would happen. It is only because I have a new perspective, not because I am against prosperous churches or people by any means.

5. *What are some practical pointers or thoughts you would like to provide those coming to the mission field?*

> Have a prayer team in place before you start. Get all of your support before you hit the field, so you don't have to go back to that. Once you're on the field, you'll want to focus on learning and ministry. *Be a learner, always!* Listen more than you talk. Learn to make good coffee and lots of it.

> Try not to be too alarmed when you realize the level of sacrifice of your time, agenda, personal preferences, and opinions. Mission work is *messy!* Be ready to suit up for battle. Consider that Natives are different from you in every way. Be ready to learn everything you can from them—their culture, mannerisms, belief systems, etc. You are not *only* here to *teach* but primarily to *learn*. Prepare yourself for the realities of suicide, sexual abuse,

mental illness, death, alcoholism, and drug addiction amongst the families you serve.

> Don't confuse a burden with a calling. The Lord burdens us with many ways to minister to those in need, such as prayer, intercession, and helping financially, just to name a few. Being called into full-time missionary work is a call of God to devote your life in full-time service to a particular group of people, *regardless of the cost*. Be willing to lay down your life day after day after day. Pray without ceasing. Count the cost *before* making the decision to go. *Love deeply!*

6.   *What are some scenarios, observations, and experiences that have been the most shocking, alarming, difficult, or just plain different for you?*

> Mud roads—rez road driving is dangerous (ayyy). Hungry and neglected children are the hardest for me to endure. The unemployment rate is very high. Hurt people hurt people. You may lose your personal material attachments, so just let go. Suicide and tragic deaths become part of a child's regular life. Teaching them to grieve is a regular part of the ministry.

> For me, of many difficulties, perhaps the most difficult was the death of a baby boy. Concerning the parents, what is so shocking to me is that they know what they need to do in order to get their kids back but can't seem to complete the programs

due to lack of transportation, support, and other resources that I take for granted every day.

➤ The fact that child sexual abuse is higher among Native American children than any other ethnic group in our country. Spousal abuse among Native women is the highest in our country. Alcoholic-related accidents are the number one cause of death on reservations. Alcoholism and drug addiction are rampant. Prejudice and racism towards Native Americans from surrounding border towns are staggering.

7. *What have you learned, experienced, or observed about Native American culture, individuals, families while working on or near our reservations?*

➤ Native women are strong, stoic, and reserved. Native people possess a wealth of love and wisdom. Grandmas are hard on their babies, but they do this to teach them to be strong. Elderly people depend on their grandkids to chop wood for their cooking and heating fires, but the grandkids often have to leave the reservation to get training and find jobs. This can leave the elderly vulnerable.

➤ Serenity. Resilience. Artisanship. Creativity.

➤ A lack of money doesn't make you poor. A small shack can be filled with more love than a mansion.

➤ Native people, customs, and families are some of the most beautiful that you will ever have the privilege to encounter. From their "teachings" to their ways of living, surviving, and thriving. If you pay attention, you can learn *many* things. They are peaceful and calm and have the best sense of humor. I mean, just plain *funny!* Though they suffer from great oppression, their resilience is awe-inspiring. Their deep-rooted love and priority of elders and family are exemplary for the rest of America.

➤ Natives are lovely and beautiful people. They love to laugh, and those who have found Christ as their personal Savior are totally on fire for God. Jesus is alive and working miracles all over the Native American nations that can and will ignite the rest of America.

8. *What should potential missionaries know or understand as it pertains to the people, culture, customs, language, and history?*

➤ Native American people won't always tell you "no" even if they think it. Listen with your eyes and ears before you speak. Learn as much language as you can. Learn about the Long Walk, the uranium mines, Dine's history. Don't be ignorant of the effects of colonialism or colonization.

➤ Watch someone make and etch and paint pottery, silversmiths that make the jewelry, and watch weavers make amazing patterns. Then you will appreciate these artisans and their incredible products. It is awe-inspiring.

> Ask questions. Never make assumptions. If you want to know why they do what they do, ask them! Embrace the *many* differences. Everything that Natives do is symbolic. From the way they wear their hair to the clothes they wear. Learn the culture. It is simply beautiful.

> COVID-19 has taken the lives of many Native pastors and evangelists. New Christian leaders need to be trained to fill the void. Our First Nations people are a sleeping giant waiting to wake to God's call and shake this whole country with the power of God!

9. *Based on some mistakes you may have made or assumptions you have held, what should potential missionaries avoid?*

> Respect private, personal space. Don't initiate hugging. Don't squeeze hands hard when you shake hands. Avoid direct eye contact for long periods of time. Be quiet when you enter a home and wait. Just wait.

> Unless you're Native American, do not use the word "Indian" to describe any people that are not from India. Do not use the word "orphan." The children have parents.

> Be humble. Be filled with the Spirit and not with yourself. Learn to feed yourself and others with the Word of God. You're not in Kansas anymore, Dorothy!

10. *When stepping onto Native American soil with a heart to serve, you can expect that...*

> Whatever your church experience has been, except that it will be all the way different. Embrace the difference with joy. Nothing will prepare you for the heartache and paradoxical joy that you will experience when you disciple someone who had no idea about God's love and the freedom we have in Christ. Seeing people mature in their walk will encourage you. If you're sad or lonely, visit an elder and ask to hear stories of their life. Visit their sheep corral. Jesus is always there.

> Spiritual warfare is daily. Expect to feel disrespected by the children and the fact that it will take time to develop your authority. This is earned over time and experience. Realize you can experience 'backlash' from the enemy. He does not want you here, he does not want these kids here, and you can expect some hardships. Stand firm in your faith and know that God is faithful. If He brought you to it, He would see you through it.

> Getting along with those you are called to work alongside can be a battle all by itself. Choose to fight for unity. Discord is simply not an option when doing kingdom work. Make a decision early on to get over yourself. The focus should always be on the children, not so much on how you are feeling. Don't get weary in well-doing. This is incredibly important work, and you *will* see a harvest if

you faint not. In short, don't throw in the towel too soon, and keep your eyes fixed on Jesus.

> God will lead you and guide you. He had gone before you and prepared the way. "Always trust in the Lord with all your heart and lean not unto your own understanding. In all of your ways, acknowledge Him, and He will direct your path."

Concluding Reflections

When Jesus was taken into the wilderness to be tempted by the devil, He addressed the adversary's temptations by responding, "It is written." He then declared to the enemy what was written (Matthew 4:1-11). How much more will we need to know what is written when tempted in our wilderness?

This next chapter provides word prayers and strategic scriptures to get planted deeply into your heart.

Prayers and Scriptures

This chapter offers prayer warriors significant scriptures related to prayer to internalize and speak out loud. Speaking the word of God in prayer on a regular basis is arguably one of the most vitally important spiritual disciplines.

We know that death and life are in the power of the tongue (Proverbs 18:21), so direct and release your faith by actively engaging in this discipline.

In *Psalm 45:1*, David said that his tongue was *as the pen of a ready writer*. And in *Proverbs 3:1, 3,* the Word states that we should not forget God's laws but write them on the tablet of our heart.

We see from these two Scriptures that our heart is the tablet, and our tongue is the pen.

When we confess God's word out loud, we write it in our own heart, and it *becomes more firmly established both in our heart and in the earth.*

Remember, we serve a God who "gives life to the dead and *calls* those things which do not exist as though they did" (Romans 4:17).

Index of Scriptures to Plant in Your Heart

"Have I not commanded you? Be strong and courageous. Do not be frightened, and do not be dismayed, for the LORD your God is with you wherever you go" (Joshua 1:9).

"For God gave us a spirit not of fear but of power and love and self-control" (2 Timothy 1:7).

"Fear not, for I am with you; be not dismayed, for I am your God; I will strengthen you, I will help you, I will uphold you with my righteous right hand" (Isaiah 41:10).

"I can do all things through him who strengthens me" (Isaiah 41:10).

"No, in all these things we are more than conquerors through him who loved us" (Romans 8:37).

"Rejoice not over me, O my enemy; when I fall, I shall rise; when I sit in darkness, the LORD will be a light to me" (Micah 7:8).

"Trust in the LORD with all your heart, and do not lean on your own understanding. In all your ways acknowledge him, and he will make straight your paths" (Proverbs 3:5-6).

"And he will be the stability of your times, abundance of salvation, wisdom, and knowledge; the fear of the LORD is Zion's treasure" (Isaiah 33:6).

"And let us not grow weary of doing good, for in due season we will reap, if we do not give up" (Galatians 6:9).

"We are afflicted in every way, but not crushed; perplexed, but not driven to despair; persecuted, but not forsaken; struck down, but not destroyed" (2 Corinthians 4:8-9).

"For I consider that the sufferings of this present time are not worth comparing with the glory that is to be revealed to us" (Romans 8:18).

"I press on toward the goal for the prize of the upward call of God in Christ Jesus" (Philippians 3:14).

"But they who wait for the LORD shall renew their strength; they shall mount up with wings like eagles; they shall run and not be weary; they shall walk and not faint" (Isaiah 40:31).

"Rejoice in hope, be patient in tribulation, be constant in prayer" (Romans 12:12).

"Therefore, my beloved brothers, be steadfast, immovable, always abounding in the work of the Lord, knowing that in the Lord your labor is not in vain" (1 Corinthians15:58).

"Blessed is the man who remains steadfast under trial, for when he has stood the test he will receive the crown of life, which God has promised to those who love him" (James 1:12).

"For you have need of endurance, so that when you have done the will of God you may receive what is promised" (Hebrews 10:36).

"He gives power to the faint, and to him who has no might he increases strength" (Isaiah 40:29).

> Blessed is the man who walks not
> in the counsel of the wicked, nor stands
> in the way of sinners, nor sits in the seat
> of scoffers; but his delight is in the law
> of the lord, and on His law he meditates
> day and night. He is like a tree planted
> by streams of water that yields its fruit in
> season, and its leaf does not wither. In all
> that he does, he prospers.
>
> Psalm 1:1

"Come to me, all who labor and are heavy laden, and I will give you rest" (Matthew 11:28).

"God is in the midst of her; she shall not be moved; God will help her when morning dawns" (Psalm 46:5).

> Therefore, since we are surrounded by so great a cloud of witnesses, let us also lay aside every weight, and sin which clings so closely, and let us run with endurance the race that is set before us, looking to Jesus, the founder and perfecter of our faith, who for the joy that was set before Him endured the cross, despising the shame, and is seated at the right hand of the throne of God. Consider Him who endured from sinners such hostility against Himself, so that you may not grow weary or fainthearted.
>
> Hebrews 12:1-3

"I know how to be brought low, and I know how to abound. In any and every circumstance, I have learned the secret of facing plenty and hunger, abundance and need" (Philippians 4:12).

"May the God of hope fill you with all joy and peace in believing, so that by the power of the Holy Spirit you may abound in hope" (Romans 15:13).

> In You, O Lord, do I take refuge; let me never be put to shame; in your righteousness deliver me! Incline your ear to me; rescue me speedily! Be a rock of refuge for me, a strong fortress to save me! For you are my rock and my fortress; and for your name's sake you lead me and guide me; you take me out of the net they have hidden for me, for you are my ref-

uge. Into your hand I commit my spirit;
you have redeemed me, O Lord, faithful
God.

Psalms 31:1-5

Prayers Filled with Scripture are Full of Power!

Jesus was a prayer warrior, spending time with His
Father daily and early. How much more must we be prayed
up? Jesus claimed, "He only did what He saw His father
doing" (John 5:19). Jesus was able to honor His Father in all
that He did because He spent time in prayer with His Father.

Reading scriptures related to prayer
is good. Talking about scripture-related
prayer is good. But *neither* accomplishes
anything if we are not actually praying.
Paul admonishes us to pray without
ceasing.

1 Thessalonians 5:17

Heavenly Father, I come boldly to
the throne of grace to obtain mercy and
find grace to help in time of need. I humble myself and repent for all of my sin.
I receive Your cleansing from all unrigh-
teousness through the blood of Your Son,
Jesus Christ. Thank You for robes of
righteousness today. Thank You for Your
amazing grace.

Hebrews 4:16, 1 John 1:9

Lord, You alone have brought me out of the power of darkness and the shadow of death, and You have broken my chains into pieces" (Psalm 107:14).

As I am being called to the front-line in this hour, I submit myself to being developed and processed in order to fulfill Your purpose (Matthew 20:16, 2 Timothy 2:20-21).

Thank You for loving me with an everlasting love. With lovingkindness You have drawn me to Yourself and You are causing me to be restored and rebuilt. Touch my lips with the coals from the altar and strengthen my voice. I will go for You.

Jeremiah 31:2-4; Isaiah 6:6-9

Lord, above all else, I desire to guard and protect my heart. Deliver me from evil and fill me with light that there be no part of me in common with darkness. I ask for a fresh perspective of Your finished work on the cross and enable me to walk in my authority in Christ. Thank You for transforming me as I continue to renew my mind to the Word of God.

Proverbs 4:23, Matthew 6:13, Luke 11:34-36, Luke 10:19, Romans 12:2

I have been called out and separated for a *special* service. Anoint my life with the fresh oil that I might arise in supernatural ability to accomplish Your will. Give me a new boldness and empowerment to stand firm as a soldier in Your army.

Isaiah 61:1, 2 Corinthians 6:17

My heart cries out to You Lord! Your Kingdom come! Your will be done! In the earth as it is in Heaven. Open my eyes to see what has been written before the foundations of the world about my life, my family, my community, my nation. Allow me to see Your plans that I might come into agreement with them and walk it out in my daily life.

Matthew 6:10, Psalm 139:16

Father, I am only able to love because You first loved me. I am asking you to fill me with a fresh infilling of the agape (love) of God from The Father. Enable me to truly demonstrate the love of God to all of whom I come into contact. Grant me the grace to forgive and let go of all offense, wounds and hurts. I choose to forgive myself as I know that guilt, shame and fear are not from You. Let the love of God be seen and felt by others that they may know that I belong to You.

> 1 John 4:19, Matthew 6:14-15, Romans 8:1, John 13:35

I choose this day to lay aside every weight and the sin which so easily ensnare me. I will arise and run with endurance the race that is set before me as I look unto Jesus, the Author and the Finisher of my faith.

> Hebrews 12:1-2

I open my heart to the power of Your word which is living and powerful, and sharper than any two-edged sword. I allow it to pierce even to the division of soul and spirit, and of joints and marrow. It is a discerner of my thoughts and the intentions of my heart.

> Hebrews 4:12

Lord, I will pay attention to Your words. I will not lose sight of them. I will keep Your message in plain view. May it penetrate deep into my innermost being and bring to life revival and renewal. Your word is precious to me; it is the healing cure, a medicine for my whole body. I will guard and blockade my heart above all else for it is the source of life and the escape from death.

> Proverbs 4:20-23

You have sent Your word and You have healed me (Psalm 107:20).

Thank You Jesus for Your finished work on the cross. By Your stripes, I am healed—spirit, soul and body. From the crown of my head to the soles of my feet, I am healed.

Isaiah 53:5

You have prepared a table for me, in the presence of my enemies (Psalm 23:5).

I take up the whole armor of God to withstand in the evil day, and having done all to stand, I will stand! I put on the helmet of salvation and the breastplate of righteousness. I gird my loins with Truth and shod my feet with the preparation of the gospel of peace. I hold up the shield of faith and I draw my sword of the spirit which is the Word of God. I pray always in every way I know through the power of the Spirit.

Ephesians 6:10-18

Woe is me for I am undone. I am a man/woman of unclean lips, and I dwell in the midst of a people of unclean lips. For my eyes have seen the King, the Lord of hosts. Lord, send Your angels with a live coal, taken with tongs from the altar. Touch my mouth with it. Take my iniquity away and purge my sinfulness. Lord, if You are looking for someone to go, if you are looking for someone to send. Here I am, Lord. Send me.

Isaiah 6:1-9

Concluding Reflections

God's Word is forever settled in heaven (Psalm 119:89), *and we establish it in the earth each time we speak it.*

I want to encourage you. Pick up your armor, soldier. The mighty sword of the spirit, the word of God, and move forward by faith.

I encourage you to make Psalm 91 personal by changing the pronouns. We know that God watches over His word to secure its performance. Praying Psalm 91 in a personal way makes it even *more* intimate and effective. It provides a powerful new perspective. The more you pray it, the more it becomes a part of your spirit. Then, when you need it the most, it will automatically flow out of you.

Praying Psalm 91 Over Yourself and Your Family

_____ dwells in the secret
place of the Most High
We shall abide under the shadow of the Almighty.
_____ will say of the Lord,
"He is my refuge and my fortress;
My God, in Him I will trust."
Surely, He shall deliver _____ from
the snare of the fowler
And from the perilous pestilence [fatal, infectious disease].
He shall cover _____ with His feathers,
And under His wings _____ shall take refuge;
His truth shall be your shield and buckler.
_____ shall not be afraid of the terror by night,
Nor of the arrow that flies by day,
Nor of the pestilence that walks in darkness,
Nor of the destruction that lays waste at noonday.
A thousand may fall at _____'s side,
And ten thousand at your right hand;
But it shall not come near _____.
Only with _____'s eyes shall (we) look,
And see the reward of the wicked.
Because _____ have made the
Lord, who is _____'s refuge,
Even the Most High, _____'s dwelling place,
No evil shall befall you _____,
Nor shall any plague come
near _____'s dwelling;
For He shall give His angels charge over _____,
To keep _____ in all (our) ways.
In their hands they shall bear (us) up,
Lest _____ dash (our) foot against a stone.

_____ shall tread
upon the lion and the cobra,
The young lion and the serpent (we)
shall trample underfoot.
"Because _____ has set his love upon
Me, therefore I will deliver (them);
I will set _____ on high,
because _____ has known My name.
_____ shall call upon Me,
and I will answer (them);
I will be with _____ in trouble;
I will deliver _____ and honor _____.
With long life I will satisfy _____,
And show (them) My salvation."

Epilogue

When I arrived at the parking lot of this ministry all those years ago, I said, "God, I will give you *one* year!" As I mentioned earlier, He did not listen. In fact, ten years—yes, I'm serious, after that statement—I found myself in a Board Meeting. Our beloved founder was retiring, and there were six sets of eyes staring at me from around the circular table. "Genevieve, will you *take over* the ministry?" While breastfeeding my youngest daughter and with tears streaming down my face, I answered, "I'll do it for *one* year."

I reiterate this to say the early years of ministry were nothing short of grueling! And moving forward has never once been easy! I had no typical sending agency to support me or concept of, much less time, to "raise my own support." It was crazy. I worked the first year for 100 dollars a month plus room and board. I then received an increase of 100 dollars a month for every year thereafter. Obviously, this will never be the case for others as we move forward in building our non-profit structure and develop as an organization.

It was that same year, 2014, that I received a call from my grandmother. I picked up the phone. "Hi, Grandma!" She, a renowned Catholic, responded, "Genevieve, I believe that God wants me to leave you the 600 acres of tribal land in South Dakota so that you can build a NAOMI House there." I *knew* God spoke that to her. As mentioned earlier in the book, a NAOMI House is needed on most reservations across America.

Shortly before my grandmother passed away at the age of ninety-three, she said to me, "Let's go to Pine Ridge." She lived in Chadron, not too far away. Next thing you know, we were in a Tribal Council Meeting where my devout grandmother presented her *vision* for a children's home. What an incredible woman indeed. The Tribal Council voted unanimously in our favor. I know that God wants us to build there and other places. I also know that *it won't be handed to us or happen accidentally*. This is one of the reasons for this book— to unpack that one statement.

For me, I can almost hear the cries of the children. But not just the children. Their mothers and families as well. I know not everybody can. We are all different and have a unique calling, carrying a unique burden. The Lord said to me, "Daughter, if you will carry My desires, interceding and believing long enough, you will eventually *birth* My desires. If you will carry it, daughter, and don't drop it, I will bring it forth."

So, for now, with my eyes securely fixed on Jesus, the Author and Finisher of my faith, I am moving forward, one step at a time. (see Photo #10 on page 244)

THE WEEPING WOMAN AND THE RETURN OF HER CHILDREN

Thus says the Lord: "A voice was heard in Ramah. Lamentation and bitter weeping. Rachel weeping for her children. Refusing to be comforted for her children. Because they are no more."

Thus says the Lord: "Refrain your voice from weeping, And your eyes from tears.

For your work shall be rewarded, says the Lord, And they shall come back from the land of the enemy. There is hope in your future, says the Lord, That your children shall come back to their own border.

Jeremiah 31:15

Photo #1

Photo #2

Photo #3

Photos #4 and #5

Photo #6

Photo #7

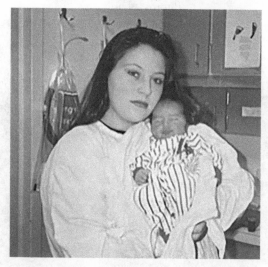

Photo #8

Photo #9

Photo #10

Appendix A

Practical Ways to Increase Your Love Walk Today

1. Invite the Holy Spirit to Cause You to Grow in Understanding of God's Love for You
   a. Diligently seek inner healing for any area of the soul that is wounded and might stand in the way of you understanding God's love for you. God's love is perfect, man's is not. We have all been through hurtful situations.
   b. We often equate God's love for us in the same way others have shown (or not shown) love towards us.
   c. We cannot let others define God's love for us.
   d. First John 4:19 says: *"We love because He first loved us."*

      The more you understand God's love for you, the more you are able to respond with love for Him and others.

2. God + Nothing = Everything You Need
   a. God + no one else = is everyone you need.
   b. When God becomes everything to you, it is easier to love, as you are secure in Him, knowing that all that you need ultimately comes from Him.

    c.   When we learn to get our needs met by Him alone, it will let everyone around us "off the hook."

    d.   It will cause us to stop living in deficiency mode and move us into a fully stocked love bank.

    e.   As a result, you will be both more loving and much easier to love.

3.   Make Love Your Greatest Aim and Focus in Life

    a.   First Corinthians 14:1 says to pursue love [to run after swiftly in order to catch or reach a goal] [to seek earnestly and eagerly].

    b.   The Message Version says: *"Go after a life of love as if your life depended on it—because it does."*

    c.   New Living Translation: *"Let love be your highest goal."*

    d.   You will empower what you focus on. Make the goal to love as God loves your highest priority, with intentionality.

4.   Be Intentional in Your Love Walk

    a.   You will have opportunities every day to choose to walk in love.

        a.   Look for opportunities.

        b.   Embrace the opportunities.

        c.   Create opportunities.

    b.   Take a look around your life, your family, your inner circle, etc.

        It won't take long, and the Holy Spirit will begin to reveal who and what situation you can practice on.

    c.   Google "random acts of kindness" ideas and do them!

  d. Remember, the purpose is to master the art of this power tool, and the best way to master something is by practice!

5. Identify Your "Grace-Growers/Love-Testers"
  a. Read, memorize, and implement Romans 12:21 in your life starting today: *"Do not become overcome with evil, but overcome (master over and win the case, defeating) evil with Good."*
  b. Identify those love testers in your life and change your attitude about them. They are your gift from God to perfect you in love.
  c. Remember, love is not provoked or irritated and does not take up offense.
  d. Offense is one of the most common tactics in the enemies' bag of tricks. DO NOT TAKE THE BATE!

6. Stop Being So Defensive!
  a. Isaiah 53:7 gives us Jesus' example. *"He was oppressed and He was afflicted, Yet He opened not His mouth; He was led as a lamb to the slaughter, And as a sheep before its shearers is silent, So He opened not His mouth."*
  b. Unless He instructs you to address or confront an issue, let the Father vindicate you.
  c. Also, be a good listener, and practice empathy.

7. Humble Yourself and Make Wrongs Right
  a. Proverbs 16:7 *"When a man's ways please the Lord, He makes even his enemies to be at peace* (safe, uninjured; to live friendly) *with him."*

    b.   The Passion Version: *When the Lord is pleased with the decisions you've made, he activates grace to turn enemies into friends.*

    c.   If you have hurt another even without meaning to, apologize and ask for forgiveness.

    d.   Humility wins many battles. It's never too late to make a wrong right.

8.   Love Those Who Hate You

    a.   Matthew 5:43-36: *"You have heard that it was said, You shall love your neighbor and hate your enemy; But I say to you, love your enemies, bless those who curse you, do good to those who hate you, and pray for those who spitefully use you and persecute you, For if you love those who love you, what reward can you have? Do not even the tax collectors do that?"*

    b.   Identify the people who are hateful to you and create ways to show them love.

9.   Be a Giver

    a.   John 3:16 *"For God so loved the world, that He gave..."*

    b.   Give of your time, giftings, prayer, and intercession.

    c.   Give material blessings, kindness, affirmations, words of love, etc.

    d.   Furthermore, DO IT CHEERFULLY:

    e.   First Corinthians 9:6-7: *"But this I say: He who sows sparingly will also reap sparingly, and he who sows bountifully will also reap bountifully. So let each one give as he purposes in his heart, not grudgingly or of necessity; for God loves [takes pleasure in, prizes above other things] a cheerful giver."*

    f.   Talk about confusing the unseen world!

10. Discern What Love "Looks Like" in Any Given Situation
    a. Sometimes love will require compassion, giving a gift, or a kind word.
    b. Sometimes love will require discipline, confrontation, and boundaries.
    c. Love will look different in different situations.
    d. For example, if someone is driving drunk, barreling down the highway at 120 mph, with a brick wall one mile ahead, "love" will pull that vehicle over at all cost and arrest the driver.
    e. *Ask God for discernment.* Love will always look to accomplish the highest good for the sake of another.
    f. The high road is not necessarily the easy road.[8]

Appendix B

Love suffers long and is kind; love does not envy; love does not parade itself, is not puffed up; does not behave rudely, does not seek its own, is not provoked, thinks no evil; does not rejoice in iniquity, but rejoices in the truth; bears all things, believes all things, hopes all things, endures all things. Love never fails...

1 Corinthians 13:4-8 (NKJV)

The Following is an Expanded Interpretive Translation of all of the Greek Words/ Definitions from 1 Corinthians 13:4-8

"Love passionately bears with others for as long as patience is needed: love doesn't demand others to be like itself but is so focused on the needs of others that it bends over backward to become what others need it to be;

Love is not ambitious, self-centered, or so consumed with itself that it never thinks of the needs or desires that others possess;

Love doesn't go around talking about itself all the time, constantly exaggerating and embellishing the facts to make it look more important in the sight of others;

Love does not behave in a prideful, arrogant, haughty, superior or snobbish manner; love is not rude or dishonoring—it is not careless or thoughtless, nor does it carry on in a fashion that would be considered insensitive to others;

Love does not manipulate situations or scheme and devises methods that will twist situations to its own advantage;

Love does not deliberately keep records of wrongs or past mistakes;

Love does not feel overjoyed when it sees an injustice done to someone else but is elated, thrilled, ecstatic, and overjoyed with the truth;

Love protects, shields, guards, covers, conceals, and safeguards people from exposure;

Love strains forward with all its might to believe the very best in every situation;

Love always expects and anticipates the best in others and the best for others;

Love never quits, never surrenders, and never gives up;

Love never disappoints, never fails, and never lets anyone down."

Love Suffers Long/Patient—*makrothymeō*
Never gives up. Bravely endures offense and injury.

Symbolizing a long duration, like a candle with a very long wick, it is prepared to burn a long time.

Love is Kind—*chrēsteuomai*
Adaptable or compliant to the needs of others.

Good-willed and benevolent, kindness delights in contributing to the happiness of the other.

Love Does Not Envy—*zēloō*
Not heated or boiling with envy and hatred.

Zelos portrays a person consumed with making their own successful way in life, willing to sacrifice anything or anyone to get it.

Agape does not want what it doesn't have, nor is it *pained* by the excellence, prosperity, or happiness of another.

Love Does Not Parade Itself—*perpereuomai*
To extol oneself excessively.

Agape is so strong, so sure, and so confident that it desires to focus on the accomplishments of others in order to build them up and make them feel more valuable and secure.

Love Is Not Puffed Up—*phusio*
To be proud, to be swollen, or to be inflated.

Knowledge puffs up with an air of superiority and haughtiness, but *agape* love edifies.

Love Does Not Behave Rudely—*aschemoneo*
To act in an unbecoming manner, suggesting
a person who is tactless or thoughtless.

Love Seeks Not Its Own—*zeteo*
So intent on getting his way that he will
search, seek, and investigate,
never giving up in his pursuit to get what he wants.

Agape is not conceited. It isn't always "me first," nor is it selfish or self-seeking.

Love Is Not Easily Provoked—*paroxsuno*
to poke, to prick, or to stick, as with a sharpened
instrument until the victim becomes provoked, resulting
in a fight—a conflict of the most serious order.

Agape is not quick-tempered or easily irritated, aggravated or annoyed

Love Thinks No Evil—*logidzomai*
An accounting term. A picture of an offended
person who keeps detailed records of every
wrong that was ever done to him.

Agape takes no account of the evil done to it, paying no attention to a suffered wrong.

Love Rejoices Not in Iniquity—But
Rejoices in the Truth—*ou chairei*
Love is elated, thrilled, ecstatic, and
overjoyed when truth reigns.

Love Bears All Things—*stego*
To cover, as a roof covers a house.

Agape serves as protection and speaks of those who will hover over you to protect you from the storms of life.

Love Believes All Things—*pisteuei*
To put one's faith or trust in something or someone.

Agape is not blind; it sees the good, the bad, and the ugly. But because agape is so filled with faith, it pushes the disconcerting, disturbing, negative realities out of the way.

This doesn't mean that *agape* ignores problems or challenges. It just makes a choice to see beyond the problems and conflicts, to strain forward to see the highest potential that resides in every person.

Love Hopes All Things—*elpidzo*
An expectation of good things. Always expects the best.

Love Endures All Things—*hupomeno*
An attitude of a person who is under a
heavy load but refuses to surrender
to defeat because he knows he is in his place.

Agape always perseveres, never looks back in the midst of tribulation or adverse circumstances, but keeps going to the end; without weakening.

Love Never Fails—*pipto*
Never falls from a high position powerless
to the ground, being without effect.

LET'S PRAY:

Lord, I want to be the embodiment of Your love. I know that I fall very short of the agape love that You desire to see operating in my life. Therefore, I am asking You to help me move upward to the highest level of love so I can be a channel through which this love can be poured out to others whom I know and meet. Just as You have loved me, help me become a life-changing source of divine love to other people. Help me to be a carrier of the power of love to those around me and walk in atmospheres of deliverance. I pray this in Jesus' name. Amen.

LET'S CONFESS:

I confess that God's love dwells in me. It flows from my heart to all those around me. People who are close to me are changed and transformed by this love that operates so mightily in me. When others see me, they think of the love of God, for it is demonstrated continually in my life. I declare this by faith in Jesus' name!

Appendix C

————◄———— >)•(< ————►————

Ten Practical Ways YOU Can Become an Educator and Advocate Today

✓ Recommend *this Book* and/or the link [www.preparingforthecall.com] to your family friends, community, church, a missions' pastor, or the next stranger you meet.

✓ Recommend *this Video* https://youtu.be/KftCK0-pP-s to your family, friends, community, church, a missions' pastor, or the next stranger you meet.

✓ Share the links to your Facebook wall, all social media outlets, and email network.

✓ "Like" us on Facebook and share our page! (https://www.facebook.com/NAOMIHouseAZ)

✓ Purchase items on Amazon and have them sent. View our Practical Needs List here: www.thenaomihouse.org/getinvolved.

✓ Send a monitory donation. Click the link to make a one-time or monthly donation. www.thenaomihouse.org/getinvolved.

✓ OR, mail a check to: NAOMI House—PO Box 205, Joseph City, Arizona 86032

✓ Subscribe! Become a member of the NAOMI House Tribe at www.thenaomihouse.org/getinvolved for regular updates.

✓ Become a prayer partner! www.thenaomihouse.org. Commit to praying for our children and staff through our Prayer Patron Program.

✓ Host a "Campaign of Awareness" gathering. This can be in your Living Room or Invite us to your church or mission's event. www.thenaomihouse.org/getinvolved.

✓ Assemble a work-group of volunteers to spend a day or three or a week on the mission field. www.thenaomihouse.org/getinvolved.

Additional Resources / E-Books

E-Books by Genevieve:
www.preparingforthecall.com/ebooks

Endnotes

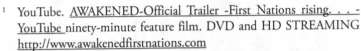

1   YouTube. AWAKENED-Official Trailer -First Nations rising. . . - YouTube ninety-minute feature film. DVD and HD STREAMING http://www.awakenedfirstnations.com
2   www.preparingforthecall.com/south-dakota
3   Youtube. *The Invasion of America.* https://www.youtube.com/ watch?v=pJxrTzfG2bo
4   This section is a paraphrase of *The American Psychological Association.* For more information on Indian Child Welfare Act of 1978, see: https://www.apa.org/pi/families/resources/newsletter/2017/12/ indian-child-welfare
5   I encourage you to watch the following links in order to better understand the remainder of this chapter: https://www.youtube.com/ watch?v=UGqWRyBCHhw (thirteen-minute video), https://www. youtube.com/watch?v=Yo1bYj-R7F0 (one-hour documentary).
6   Gloria Brinthall, *Stuff Happens: H.O.P.E. Anyway* https://www.amazon. com/Stuff-Happens-H-P-Anyway-ebook/dp/B07Z8D4C5Q/ ref=sr_1_1?dchild=1&keywords=gloria+brintnall &qid=1628267221&sr=8-1
7   *The following informational video can be viewed at https://www.youtube. com/watch?v=J-HYCWTpKPE&t=717s*
8   *Winning Your Battles in Life with God's Love, by Patricia King Ministries*—used with permission

About the Author

Genevieve is a mother, non-profit director, public speaker, author, and child advocate. Knowing first-hand the power of God to deliver from darkness, she has an insatiable passion to see others *find freedom and discover purpose.*

She is teaching the life-changing message of hope and fullness of redemption found in Christ.

Genevieve has a desire to educate others about Native American children and their need for Safe Houses on Reservations. She is also sharing the story of hope and movement of the Spirit of God upon the First Nations people and how it will impact America and the Nations.

She was married in 2008. Her son, Josh, is an Army Veteran and police officer. Genevieve resides in Northern Arizona with her twelve-year-old daughter, Shenoa, her seven-year-old daughter, Aliza, and cat Rajah Blu.

For more information, please go to: www.preparingforthecall.com
Facebook: www.facebook.com/ GenevieveDawnS
Instagram: @genevievedawns